Lost Worlds of Africa

By the same author

THE GREAT SAHARA

JAMES WELLARD

Lost Worlds of Africa

NEW YORK
E. P. DUTTON & CO., INC.
1967

In memory of my father

 / Library of Congress catalog card number: 67-20536 / First Edition.

CONTENTS

ILLUSTRATIONS

MAPS

PREFACE

This book is a sequel to the author's *The Great Sahara* which recounted in general terms the history of the Desert from prehistoric times to the present. *Lost Worlds of Africa*, which is the outcome of further travels and research, is an attempt to give a more detailed picture of certain aspects of African life which were not fully discussed or developed in the previous book.

The single traveller without the resources of a well-organised expedition cannot do more than cover a very limited area, give his personal impressions of what he actually sees, and advance theories based on his limited experience. He can, however, take some comfort from the fact that the bulk of the literature of Africa is of this kind, for until quite recently the continent had only been explored by individual travellers and revealed to the West through their narratives. Nowadays, exploration of even the most inaccessible regions of the earth are organised on a very different scale from the small caravans of the early explorers, and one must admit that the day of the 'African travellers', as Heinrich Barth and that whole company of nineteenth-century pioneers modestly described themselves, is, to all intents and purposes, over.

However, there is no regulation that prevents the private individual from following in the footsteps of Hornemann, Laing, Caillié, Barth, and Richardson, and it is sometimes advantageous to 'travel light', as they did. The Dawada, for instance, cannot be reached by expeditions in wheeled vehicles; hence no thorough 'scientific' study of these isolated survivors of some ancient civilisation has yet been made. In the meantime, until they have their skulls measured and snippets of their skin sent back to the laboratories of the universities, they must be reported upon in much the same manner as they were described by Walter Oudney, the first European traveller to see them some 150 years ago.

I was able to visit the Dawada and to give the account of them which will be found in the following pages thanks to the kind help of His Excellency Haj el Faki ben Kedaze, the Tuareg Governor of Ubari. Concurrently, Dr. M. S. Ayoub, Controller of Antiquities for the Fezzan, and the Mudir of el Greifa, Abdel Rassig, generously organised for me the small camel caravan which enabled me to go into the Ramla. I now take this opportunity of formally thanking all three officials, together with the headmen of the Dawada villages where I stayed during my journey.

My visit to the Acacus Mountains in south-west Libya was made possible by the co-operation of the Royal Air Force whose Desert Rescue group, formerly based at Idris, Tripoli, invited me to accompany them on an exercise to this still-unexplored region of the Sahara. As a member of the Desert Rescue's team, I was able to study and photograph prehistoric rock drawings which have not, as far as I know, ever been reported upon in an English publication. At the same time, I hasten to add that the Acacus has been the scene of some ten years' dedicated study by my friend Dr. Fabrizio Mori, whose *Tadrart Acacus* (see Bibliographical Notes, Book Two, Chapters Four–Six) gives a detailed and authoritative account of these magnificent art galleries.

I owe special thanks to the Commander and officers of R.A.F. Idris for their generous help and hospitality; and to Lieutenant-Colonel Walter Hingston, editor of *The Geographical Magazine*, for his advice and encouragement. Acknowledgements are also made to Colonel Hingston for permission to use some material first published in *The Geographical Magazine* following my visit to the Acacus.

Articles and photographs collected during my journeys in Africa were commissioned by the *Weekend Telegraph* (London) and *Horizon* magazine (New York), and I wish to thank the proprietors and editors of these periodicals for permission to reproduce extracts and illustrations from material submitted to them.

I also record my thanks to the staff of the Reading Room of the British Museum and other libraries that I have used; to the directors of museums in Europe and Africa; to the heads of various Departments of Tourism and Antiquities; and to the authors and publishers of those books and journals which I have referred to in detail in the Bibliographical Notes appended to this volume.

The Index was made by my daughter, Julia, to whom my thanks.

A word (as is usual with books about Africa) is needed regarding the orthography of place names, since considerable confusion results from the variety of spellings, due to the Arabic, French, German or English versions of one and the same place. An additional complication is caused by changes in even the English spelling of a town from one period to another. Timbuktu (Timbuctoo, Tomboktu, et cetera) and Salé (Salee, Sali, Sally) are obvious examples; and when it comes to the oasis of Ouargla in Algeria, once an important religious centre of the Berbers, the writer is confronted with the following choice of spellings: Wargla, Guerguela, Wurglah, Wargalah, Wurgelah, Guargala, Huerguela, Ouergelah, and several others. However, as far as possible, place names in this book have been given their current English forms as found in English atlases and dictionaries. Even so, the reader's indulgence has to be asked if the spelling he prefers has not been used.

Unless otherwise credited, all the illustrations are from photographs taken by the author.

INTRODUCTION

Terra Incognita

We know nothing of the personal life of the great astronomer Claudius Ptolemaeus except that he lived in Alexandria in Egypt. But it has been observed that an astronomer always leaves his date in his works; hence we can be almost certain that Claudius Ptolemaeus, better known as Ptolemy, was making celestial observations in A.D. 139. His astronomical treatise, *The Syntax of Astronomy*, was therefore published soon afterwards, and his *Geography*, which is partly based on these observations, in about A.D. 150–60. The science of cartography may be said to date from this time, for Ptolemy's work contains the tables of latitude and longitude on which world atlases were based for the next thousand years and on which geographers continued to rely for their maps of Africa until modern times.

By the middle of the nineteenth century we still did not know where the Nile had its source or in what direction the Niger River flowed, since Ptolemy was thought to be unreliable on both questions. His statement that 'the snows of the Mountain of the Moon are received by the lakes of the Nile' was not credited, on the grounds that no mountains located so near the equator (Ptolemy places them at Lat. 12°30′) could be snow-capped. The discovery of Mount Kilimanjaro (Lat. 3°) in 1848 suggested that the Alexandrian astronomer was almost correct. As regards the river he calls 'Nigir', geographers have never been able to agree whether he is describing the great stream south of the Sahara Desert or some lesser North African river. In any case, it seemed inconceivable that a lone geographer working in a provincial Roman city 1,700 years before could map a region of the earth's surface that no European explorer had managed to reach.

As a result of the last 150 years of intensive exploration, however, the cartography of Africa is almost complete and Ptolemy's atlas has been superseded by aeronautical charts of 1:1,000,000. Even so, these large-scale maps, made with all the skills and instruments available to modern science, still show vast areas marked with the notations 'Relief data incomplete', or 'Mountain ranges reported', just as Ptolemy's maps mark regions south of latitude 10° *terra incognita*. All such notations are an admission that the atlases, whether second-century Greek or twentieth-century American, do not really tell us what these regions of the earth's surface actually look like.

As with the geography of Africa, so with its history, though even more so, since it is easier to draw a map than to reconstruct the past. True, a long succession of explorers, in addition to charting mountains, deserts, rivers, and inhabited places, have also reported on what they saw of human activities. But few Europeans have ever been able to see Africa through African eyes, and there are obvious reasons for their failure to do so, even in the case of those like Isabelle Eberhardt, who tried, with what amounted almost to desperation, to identify herself with the natives; or of Father de Foucauld, who lived and died in the Hoggar Mountains in the middle of the Sahara.[1]

Yet most of what we know of the Africa that lies hidden behind the façade of Western colonialism is still based on the writings of the early explorers, scholars, and mystics, though their reports, too, leave whole areas which must still be regarded as *terra incognita*: that is, worlds which have not yet been fully discovered or are actually on the verge of being lost altogether. Because of the speed and inevitability of modernisation, this 'secret' Africa seldom reveals itself to Western visitors passing by jet plane from one capital to

1. For an account of Isabelle Wilhelmine Marie Eberhardt, see *Mes Journaliers*, 1923. For other explorers of the Sahara Desert, James Wellard, *The Great Sahara*, 1964, chapters 7–13.

another, and it is liable to disappear altogether before it can be recorded. The traveller today who hopes, therefore, to catch a glimpse of what the first explorers saw must follow as best he can in their footsteps, which will take him far from the international airports into those regions marked 'Relief data unknown' on the maps.

The purpose of this book, then, is to examine certain aspects of the African world which are largely disregarded in the official fact-finding and statistical surveys, or ignored altogether in contemporary newspaper reports. Five topics have been chosen as suggestive of the totality of African culture and, it is hoped, as contributory to an understanding of its history.

The first subject is intended to illustrate the actual physical remoteness of a great part of Africa from the Western world, not only in space, but in time and spirit. It describes a people who have been isolated so long that they have become a 'lost world' in themselves, surviving into the twentieth century, but surely not capable of surviving much longer. The people chosen are not, however, primitives or 'living fossils', like the Bushmen of the Kalahari Desert, the pygmies of Central Africa, or the Aborigines of Australia. The Dawada of the Libyan Fezzan are, on the one hand, civilised and, on the other, shut off from practically all contact with civilisation. If they are the last survivors of the aboriginal North African Negro they are a link between prehistory and recorded times, and this is what makes them additionally significant to the Africanist. By the same token, they illustrate the complicated problem of social evolution which confronts Africa, for are they to be left to eke out their wretched existence in their enormous prison of sand? Or can and should they be incorporated into the society of present-day Libya?

The second topic of 'unknown' Africa deals with the earliest depictions of human life as they are found in the vast 'art galleries' scattered all over the continent. Many of these pictorial records have still not been explored, perhaps not even found. They extend over a period of 10,000 years and illustrate the manners and customs of successive epochs. Yet despite these proofs that Africans evolved at first along almost identical lines with the white race, we are inclined to think of African art as primitive, not to say barbaric, since we know it only in the form of masks, statuettes, weapons, and sundry grotesque artifacts which strike us as indicative of the cultural inferiority of those who made them. An acquaintance with the rock paintings and engravings found all over Africa must modify our assessment of the African's aesthetic and intellectual capabilities, just as our discovery of European cave art changed our ideas of our own ancestors. Thus we no longer think of those ancient hunters as ape-like creatures incapable of intellectual and spiritual refinement. So, too, the rocks of the Tassili-n-Ajjer, of the Acacus, of the Tibesti, and, in fact, the entire African continent should alter our conventional picture of the aboriginal African as a woolly-headed savage. The rock 'galleries' tell a very different story and suggest by implication that the continent which produced these artists is capable, given the time and opportunity, of rivalling and perhaps surpassing the achievements of the West.

The third subject examines one of those mysterious empires which is 'lost' to the extent that its existence has even been denied altogether. Yet the Empire of the Garamantes not only flourished for a thousand years, but reminds us that Africans were living in cities at a time when northern Europeans were inhabiting wattle huts. The Garamantes appeared far more civilised to the Romans who conquered them than the Britons or Germans, and a Roman historian describes their capital as 'very well-known'.[1] The Garamantes, moreover, appear on the scene at one of the most interesting phases of African history, only to disappear as mysteriously as they came. The world they left behind has yet to be fully explored, though its cities, watch-towers, chariot routes, and immense hydraulic

1. '*Garama, oppidum clarissimun.*' Pliny, *Natural History* V, 5.

works remain as evidence of their rôle in the making of Africa.

The traveller who stands in the ruins of a fifth-century Christian basilica in the Sahara Desert, or of a sixteenth-century Portuguese cathedral in the Congo, or, for that matter, of a modern church in some North African city, must soon become aware that he is glimpsing the vestiges of still another lost world—that of early Christianity in Africa. Between the first and last of these Christian temples lie eighteen centuries of effort to incorporate the vast land mass into Christendom. The relative lack of success, despite the enormous cost in lives and treasure, tells us a great deal about the minds and hearts of Africans. Certainly all efforts to establish Christianity in Africa north of the equator—including the first and greatest attempt during the Roman period—have failed: Islam has been the victor in the long struggle for the African's religious allegiance. Moreover, as an inevitable consequence of a bloody and merciless war, fought for over a thousand years, often on the field of battle itself, Islam and Christendom have been implacable enemies. The hundreds of Christian missionaries and travellers who died in Africa during the conquest, exploration, and proselytisation of that continent testify to that enmity. Nowadays the individual traveller, alone in even fanatically Moslem territory, is in no danger, as Mungo Park was, of being murdered as a 'Christian dog', for the simple reason that Moslems are convinced of the superiority of their faith and consider they have evidence to prove it. The material evidence is seen in the shape of thousands of Christian churches that lie scattered in ruins all over the land, frequented now only by shepherds and known only to the archaeologists. We ask ourselves why a religion, once so firmly rooted in the soil of Africa, now survives as a fairly recent European importation.

The fifth subject of this study is slavery, since that institution is endemic to Africa. Despite the fact that the enslavement of men was, until recently, world-wide and, in fact, one of the main pillars of society among all races, creeds, and nationalities, the identification of the institution with Africa is understandable in view of the enormity of the traffic involved. It is conservatively estimated that 100,000,000 Negroes were shipped out as slaves between 1441 when the trade began and 1888 when it officially ended.

It is for these reasons that we tend to think of slavery in terms of long processions of Africans yoked together as they marched through jungles or across deserts to be delivered to their overseas markets. It is such a familiar theme, and one that redounds so patently to the shame of the white man, that we tend to forget that men have always enslaved each other, and continue to do so. Moreover, during the four hundred years of the African slave trade as operated by Europeans, hundreds of thousands of Christians were enslaved by Africans, a chapter of history that seems to have been erased from men's memories by the horrors of the greater evil. It represents, however, another aspect of the Africa that has, in a sense, been lost, even though it was an important factor in shaping the history of the continent. Slavery—the traffic going in both directions—resulted in wars of conquest; and conquest resulted in wars of liberation. Hence, even if the age-old institution is now hidden under the façade of the new nationalism, the causes and effects remain. The observer will no longer see, of course, those long lines of men, women, and children being marched to the slave ports under the whips of their master. Neither, for that matter, will he see the underground dungeons, called *bagnios*, where Christian slaves like Cervantes were imprisoned.

The conclusion is that all these events, together with the times and places which gave rise to them, are factors in the making of modern Africa, even though the five subjects chosen to be discussed in the following pages belong to a past which has either receded almost beyond our ken or is about to be submerged in the onrush of contemporary developments. There is still time, however, to catch a last glimpse of the continent of Herodotus, Pliny, Ptolemy, and the first European explorers. The description 'Lost Worlds', therefore, is comparable in this historical context with the geographers' expression *terra incognita*; and if this survey is successful in filling in some of the lacunae, in time as well as in space, its purpose will have been achieved.

One other word needs to be added. The theories and suggestions put forward in this study of five phases of African culture are, in many instances, wholly subjective. While they are based on several years' travel and research, they are not presented as the findings of a specialist; to the contrary, they are merely offered as guide-posts to those regions of Africa which still remain to be explored and mapped out by professional geographers, historians, and archaeologists. It is the hope of the author that this book will at least give a glimpse of what we are looking for.

BOOK ONE

'The Forgotten of God'

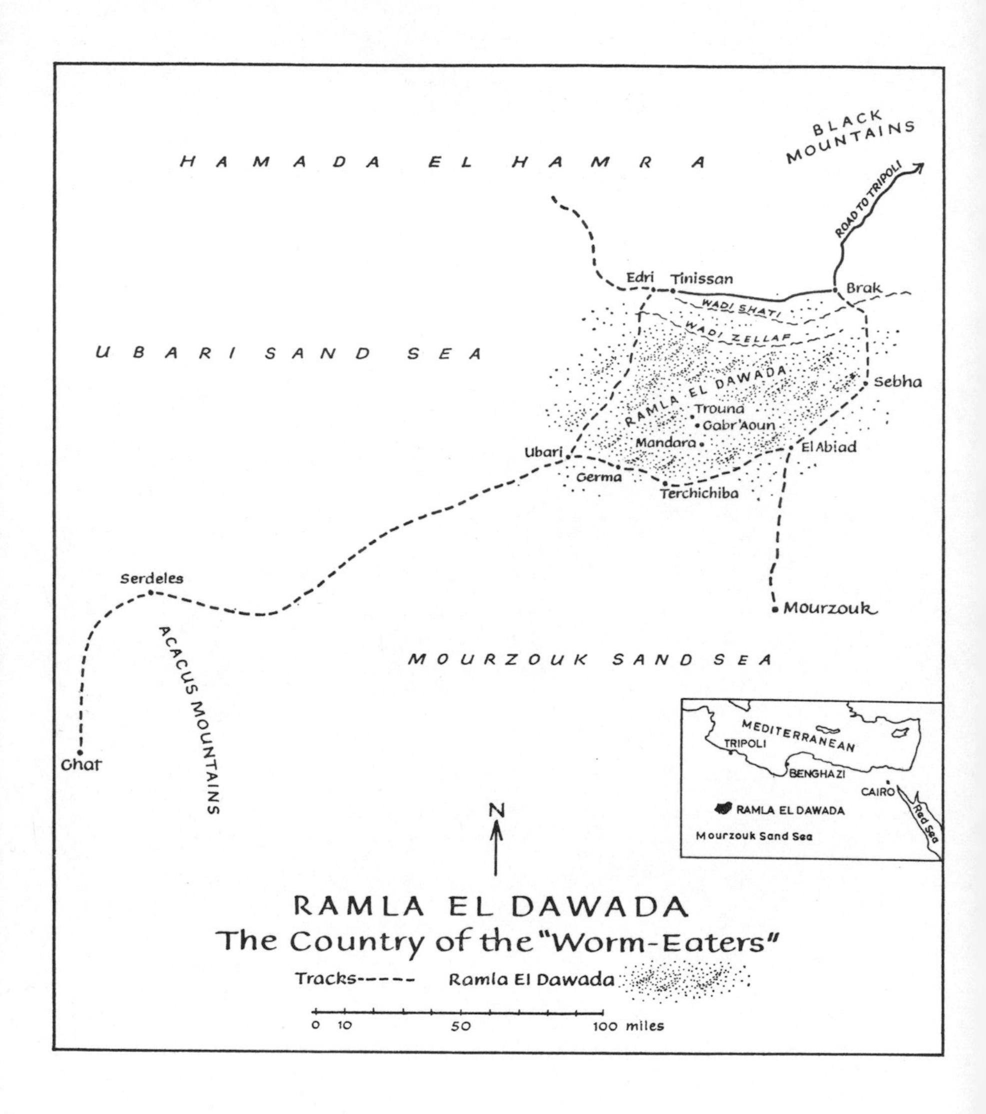
HAMADA EL HAMRA
BLACK MOUNTAINS
ROAD TO TRIPOLI
Edri
Tinissan
Brak
WADI SHATI
WADI ZELLAF
UBARI SAND SEA
RAMLA EL DAWADA
Sebha
Trouna
Gabr'Aoun
Mandara
El Abiad
Ubari
Germa
Terchichiba
Serdeles
Mourzouk
ACACUS MOUNTAINS
MOURZOUK SAND SEA
Ghat
MEDITERRANEAN
TRIPOLI
BENGHAZI
CAIRO
Red Sea
RAMLA EL DAWADA
Mourzouk Sand Sea
N
RAMLA EL DAWADA
The Country of the "Worm-Eaters"
Tracks-----
Ramla El Dawada
0 10
50
100 miles

I *Into the Sand Sea*

During one of my sojourns in the Libyan Fezzan I had frequently heard of a tribe called the Dawada, or, to give the name its literal Arab translation, the 'Worm Eaters'. According to the people of the oases, the Dawada lived beyond the enormous dunes which stretched for fifty miles along the north side of the Wadi el Ajal.

This Wadi el Ajal is a long valley running roughly south-west from Sebha, the capital of the Fezzan, to Ghat, one of the most important oases on the trans-Saharan caravan route from the Niger River to the Mediterranean coast. The valley itself is the richest historical and archaeological zone in the Sahara, for its extraordinary variety of monuments reveal 10,000 years of history. One chapter of that history which has not been fully told or explained concerned these Dawada, who had been isolated from the outside world for an undetermined number of centuries. They, apparently, had never been able to get out of their formidable sand sea. My problem was how to get in.

One realised what was involved standing on top of the first dune that marked the southern limit of their country. From this observation post, the scene is at once the most beautiful and awesome that the imagination can conceive. It is a land-scape indescribably desolate, composed of sand-hills which rise ever higher in razor-sharp ridges until they appear to reach the height of distant mountains. Not a blade of grass or any living thing is to be seen in this enormous desolation, and unless one knew otherwise, one would be forced to conclude that there was no possibility of human life beyond the towering hills of sand.

Somewhere inside this desert lived the Dawada, a small pocket of people who must have been driven into this wilderness by invaders, possibly during the pre-Roman period. Here they were at least safe, and here they had been able to survive, thanks to their lakes and ponds, some of which contained the famous 'worms' which were reported to form their principal food.

But while these remnants of the aboriginal population were safe from invaders inside their desert, they were by the same token condemned to an existence of extreme poverty, for only the means of basic survival are available to them: that is, water and barely enough food to sustain life. And just as the mountains of sand (so steep that even camels cannot cross them except through the 'valleys') protected the Dawada from their enemies, so the same barriers made escape from their prison almost impossible. They were, and are, condemned to live and die in their miniature oases in the middle of nowhere.

I learnt from my friends in the Wadi el Ajal that nobody ever went into this region except the Tuareg who visited the three Dawada villages once a year to barter a few necessities (i.e. cigarettes, flour, and olive oil) for the natron and the 'worms' the Dawada harvested in their lakes. The natron is a deposit of carbonate of soda found in many of the lakes of Africa where evaporation leaves the mineral salts baked into slabs on the foreshore. Natron was once extensively used in industry for tanning leather as well as in the baking of unleavened bread. The 'worms', on the other hand, were said to be prized by the Fezzanese as an aphrodisiac. Both products, therefore, were exportable commodities, hence the annual visit of the Tuareg caravans.

I learnt also that the Dawada were a people of the direst poverty, owning nothing but their *zeribas*, or thatched huts, a pot or two for cooking, a few little vegetable gardens, several hundred date palms, some donkeys, and the rags in which they clothed themselves. They were, moreover, not only poor, but were despised by the Fezzanese of the contiguous oases. It was not for nothing that they regarded themselves as 'the forgotten of God'.

For these and other reasons the local governor from whom I had to obtain permission to visit the Dawada was not happy about my going, and he pointed out that I was about to cross the sand sea in the month of March, which was the time of winds. But I suspected that his principal misgivings were that a visitor from the outside world could not possibly understand the reasons for the 'Worm Eaters'' isolation. He was very much aware, too, that these people were wretched in both their lives and their appearance, and he did not want me to go away with the impression that they were representative of the new Libya. However, I was able to assure the governor that my interest was historical and that I did not mind risking the sand storms. On learning that my guide was Abdul Rassig, the *modir* of the oasis of El Greifa, His Excellency (for so he is addressed) agreed to let me go.

I had first met Abdul Rassig in the village school. The school in a Fezzanese oasis is the centre of all civic and social activities, as it is the only building large enough to accommodate the score or so of men who turn up whatever the nature of the business to be transacted. The teaching staff usually comprises schoolmasters who sign on for three years' duty in these remote outposts, during which time their only contact with the outside world is a transistor radio. The schools themselves are one-storeyed whitewashed buildings, divided into a couple of classrooms and sleeping quarters for the teachers. As neither the wives of the schoolteachers, nor the mothers of the children, nor any other women are allowed inside the schoolhouse, domestic arrangements are about what one would expect to find in a frontier fort. The principal social activity is a protracted tea-and-talk ceremony in the evening, and it was during this ritual that my visit to the Dawada was discussed by the chief citizens of the oasis.

I was conscious as we sat on the floor round the tea-tray that the man who was to be my guide was observing me closely. So, I imagined, did the caravan masters examine the first nineteenth-century African travellers whom they had agreed to conduct across the Sahara, no doubt wondering whether such a visitor from another world could withstand the ordeal of long desert marches. The risk in those days, of course, was much greater on both sides, since the guide was responsible for the safety of the traveller, and the traveller, for his part, was a Christian attempting to penetrate a fanatically hostile Moslem country. The number of early explorers who were murdered in the Great Desert bears witness to the dangers and difficulties.

But all this is ancient history, and I had complete confidence in Abdul Rassig, since the governor had approved of him. As he sat in that circle of hooded men he did not strike me as either an ingratiating or even sociable companion, though I had long since learnt that the men of the desert are cautious and reticent with strangers. So I was not able to tell much from Abdul's appearance, since all that was visible of him under his cowl and cloak were his dark, serious eyes, hooked nose, and grey beard—or stubble, rather, for very few Fezzanese grow a full beard. I was to learn later what a devoutly religious man he was, of what high principles and character, though a stern taskmaster whose experience of, and attitude towards, the desert were those of the professional sailor to the sea. I discovered how severe he could be after we had been on the march for several hours on our journey the next day, when he rode his camel up alongside me about noon, tapped me on the shoulder, and told me rather sharply that I was wandering and must stay awake. I had not meant to doze, but the monotony of the vast and empty landscape and the hypnotic motion of the camel had started me dreaming. My guide was right. This was no place or time to fall asleep. To topple off one's camel could be disastrous, not so much to the rider as to the goatskin bags of water which he might bring down with him. Abdul did not smile when he reprimanded me. In fact, I never saw him smile or heard him laugh. But when, at the end of our journey, he saw that I was very tired plodding up the last long dune beyond which lay 'civilisation', he took my hand and gently encouraged me, saying that there was not much farther to go.

Abdul Rassig was nearly seventy years old.

Our caravan which went into the Ramla el Dawada consisted of Abdul the guide, Ali a camel boy, myself, and two camels, Zaila and Behir. Zaila was a large brown animal and a hard worker; Behir was white and not a good camel at all. He had been grunting and groaning ever since we set out and had hardly been able to climb the first ridge, but had sunk to his knees in the soft sand and advanced in that position. I sympathised with him, for I had had to clamber up the dune in the same undignified manner.

The sand sea in which the 400 or so surviving 'Worm Eaters' live is not, I discovered, a desert in the expected sense. It is a region of limestone mountains which have been eroded down to the living rock and then burnt by the sun and blasted by the winds into enormous ranges of pure yellow sand. Even with camels, travel in these dunes is not a simple business of marching in line across the sand. For as soon as you climb to the top of the first ridge you are in a lunar landscape. All around, as far as you can see, there is range after range of sand-hills—valleys, long slopes, cliffs, and razor-sharp peaks. The colours are deep orange, daffodil yellow, and, as the sun climbs overhead, almost white. Later the colours will change to violet and burnt umber. In the moonlight they will be silver.

There is no opportunity, however, to stand and gaze at this fantastic landscape, for camels and men alike must concentrate on the job of getting up the long slopes. Sometimes the camels are unable to advance until a zig-zag path up the sides of the dune are stamped out for them. Then, when they do reach the summit, they may be confronted with an almost perpendicular drop of several hundred feet. The caravan has to move cautiously along the crest of the cliff to find a way down; and, with care, the camels are prevented from rolling over and losing their load.

The greatest danger, however, is loose sand. My guide, like his camels, was highly suspicious of certain bright orange spots. Near to them he would pause, advance very slowly, and poke at the sand with his stick, picking up handfuls to examine and even to smell. If he was dissatisfied with the surface we would make a wide detour. In this way, in silence except for the groaning of Zaila and Behir, we advanced into the Ramla el Dawada.

In view of the difficulties of the terrain, it is not surprising that less than a score or so of Europeans have ever visited these isolated people; and the only description available in English is that of Dr. Walter Oudney, who visited them in June 1822.

Dr. Oudney was one of three Britons—the other two were Major Dixon Denham 'of His Majesty's 17th Regiment of Foot' and Captain Hugh Clapperton of the Royal Navy—who were the first Europeans ever to pass through the Fezzan and reach Lake Chad. Dr. Oudney, who died in Nigeria in 1824, left some notes of his visit to the Dawada. He writes under the date Saturday, June 29th, 1822:

> Clapperton was sitting on the top of a high hill, and so pleased with the view that he called out several times for me to dismount from my camel to enjoy the treat. The appearance was beautiful . . . There is something pretty in a lake surrounded with date palms; but when every other object is dreary, the scene becomes doubly so.
>
> The worms celebrated in this kingdom are found in these lakes.

My view of the first of the lakes came after five hours' march when we breasted the sixth and last sand ridge and looked down on an oval sheet of water, lilac and sapphire-blue in colour and encircled by dark-green palm trees—the breathtakingly beautiful sight which Captain Clapperton had summoned his companion to enjoy nearly 150 years ago.

'Mandara!' said my guide with understandable pride, for to find this lake and the village beside it in this ocean of sand was a triumph of desert navigation. But, as Dr. Oudney discovered, no words can describe the traveller's sensations on suddenly seeing this miniature jewel in the middle of such desolation; and, as if understanding my feelings, Abdul the guide allowed me to sit down and gaze my fill. Otherwise, one does not stop on a desert march, and if somebody falls behind it is up to him to catch up—unless he is sick or, like me, an outsider. True, I had already experienced what it meant to be left behind, for at one point on our journey the loose pages of the Koran which Abdul had tied up in his face-scarf had blown away, and both he and Ali the camel boy had scurried off over the dunes in pursuit, leaving me with two camels and no idea where I was for a very long quarter of an hour.

Between them they retrieved all the lost pages.

But this, of course, was different. We had nearly reached our journey's end, and I could watch my caravan winding down the long slope towards the village. After a while I began the last lap of a long walk, descending the dune to the lake. As I approached, I saw the habitations of the Dawada scattered about the sand-hills—huts called *zeriba* made of the fronds of palms set down in the sand. I saw, too, the tiny gardens watered by wickerwork baskets lowered on the trunks of palm trees weighted at one end by chunks of natron. Of the people I as yet saw nothing. They had apparently fled at the sight of visitors from the outside world.

My guide was waiting for me, and he now led me to the hut of the headman, who appeared from an adjacent cabin. He was an elderly man, with skin the colour and texture of slate, a white moustache, and a short grizzled beard, the patriarchal representative of a race, or tribe, of Negroes whose origin and history are absolutely unknown.

My host received me with handshakes, smiles, and those endless formula-phrases which are *de rigueur* in Arabic-speaking countries. In any case, my Arabic is restricted to the exchange of these courtesies, and I was glad when a villager who had worked in Tripoli and spoke a rudimentary Italian was called in to act as interpreter. I was shown into a hut where a blanket had been spread on the sand floor. Here we sat, smiling and nodding; more village dignitaries appeared at the door, crouched, came inside, sat on their haunches, and the tea ceremony typical of Libyan hospitality began. A plaited dish cover of dates was set on the floor in the middle of the circle; the headman personally squeezed them and rubbed off the sand between his palms before presenting me with the most succulent; and the ritual of welcome which was to last from sunset to midnight commenced.

During the course of the evening, I had my first taste of the famous 'worms'.

The 'worm', or *dood* as it is called, is actually a sort of brine shrimp, the scientific name of which is *Artemia salina*. It is blood-red in colour, black-headed, about a sixth of an inch long, and lives in three of the lakes which are found in the sand-dunes. Since the water of these lakes is heavily charged with carbonate of soda, or natron, and is comparable in taste and density with the water of the Dead Sea, how any creature can exist in such a strong brew is a mystery. And how did they get into these lakes in the first place?

Next morning I went down to the Lake of Mandara to try to find out something about them. When I reached the edge, the water was wine-red with billions of these animalcules, carried along by the current and, at the same time, propelling themselves hither and yon, feeding on whatever it is that nourishes them. They swirl around with the wind and current like crimson frog-spawn. Thousands of them had become stranded on the salt crust at the verge of the lake. I picked one up. It resembled a small blob of red jelly. On closer examination I saw that Dr. Oudney's description was correct: the 'worm' was a miniature crustacean 'with a strong slimy smell; the eyes two large spots supported on two long peduncles; the body a row of rays on each side, like the fins of fishes'. I filled a bottle with a fair-sized sample, intending to bring my catch back to London for microscopic examination. But I must confess that the odour became so unbearable after two days that I abandoned my bottle. I was afraid I wouldn't be allowed through the Customs!

In the meantime, while I was down at the lake, the women and girls had begun the day's fishing. I had already inferred from what the headman told me that there was some ritual or tabu associated with *dood*-fishing, for only the women and girls are allowed to enter the lake, and only on alternate days. In addition, no woman can go into the water until forty-one days after childbirth, after she has been purified by incense.

In order to ensure a good supply of 'fish', all the females who can walk are employed in the endless drudgery of pushing their seines through the shallows, netting the 'worms' in eight-foot-long muslin bags attached to a long handle which they sweep back and forth through the water. They go round and round with no more expression and probably no more feelings than if they were on a treadmill. Obviously this form of 'dredging' requires no skill whatsoever—only the patience and endurance the Arab expects of his donkey. According to Dr. Oudney, it was the men who fished in his day—though he may not have actually seen the operation. Today the soul-destroying job has been allocated to the women and evidently justified by some religious sanction. But whatever the ritualistic implications, the drudgery of pushing a net through the water all day long is still a form of serfdom; and judging by the expression of the faces of the women as they pass by, muffled up in their rags (the water is icy-cold), they know it.

One can best appreciate this by standing on the sandy shore and looking out across the lake. Where the 'worms' swarm, the surface is sunset red. In the centre it is almost purple, because, the Dawada say, it is bottomless. The women must be careful, therefore, to avoid the deep places and to wend their way by experience and instinct through the shallows.

When I inquired how deep these lakes were, I was told that nobody knew. As the Dawada have no boats of any description and the men are forbidden to enter the water, they have no way of knowing. A sounding of the lakes cannot be made until some explorer gets through with a collapsible boat.

Another mystery is where the water comes from. It scarcely ever rains in the Fezzan—sometimes not a drop of water falling for ten years at a time. Yet there is abundant water. I was taken to one lake which, though deserted and forbidding in its silence, was the most beautiful of all. Lake Amouna measures about a quarter of a mile long and sixty yards wide and is set in the middle of high dunes whose sandy sides descend precipitously 200 feet down to the water. How, one asks, do these sand walls contain a lake? Moreover, at a distance of two feet from the edge of the lake, the villager who took me to see this place scooped out the sand with his hands and up welled a pool of water which, though brackish, was still fit to drink. Yet the water in the lake itself is so full of minerals that not even the 'worms' can live in it.

There are, naturally, many legends about these lakes, for it has to be explained how they can keep their level in mid-summer as well as in winter—in one of the hottest regions of the world. The geographers have various untested explanations involving the Sahara watersheds and underground reservoirs. The Dawadas rely on their myths. One says that a plate dropped into the lake at Gabr'aoun eventually reappeared in a well at Istanbul. It is difficult to understand what they are driving at. Another legend says the lakes were caused by huge stones falling from the sky—evidently a reference to meteorites. Still a third reports the quivering and filling of the lakes when sudden explosions are heard inside the dunes.

But whatever the legends of the Dawadas and the theories of the geographers, the abundance of water is astonishing. While crossing the actual desert, far from the lakes and villages, my guide would occasionally point to a sand cliff and inform me that there was a well up there in a location where one would have said it was inconceivable.

Three of the ten lakes, then, contain the *dood* which, with dates, form the staple diet of the 'Worm Eaters'. The crustacean is eaten in the form of dried fish-cakes after being mashed up, dried in the sun, and stored in the sand. Its appearance after these processes is that of a piece of dried mud. Its smell can only be described as stinking caviar. A lump was offered to me and, in the cause of science, I broke off a piece, removed the hairs, and ate it with appropriate sounds of enjoyment, as became a guest. Its taste was not quite as evil as its look or smell, but I doubt whether there will ever be much demand for it in European restaurants.

The Dawada also heat up their 'worms' with olive oil and tomato purée (if they have any), mash up their pollenta bread in it, and eat it as a sort of pudding. Since everybody 'at table' on the occasion of my visit thrust his right hand into the bowl to expedite the process, I suddenly discovered that I was no longer hungry. My hosts were seriously alarmed by my want of appetite.

The worm cakes, incidentally, were once well thought of in the Fezzan as an aphrodisiac and their export by means of the annual Tuareg caravan that visited the Dawada villages enabled the 'Worm Eaters' to get cash to buy a few luxuries from the outside world.

The other source of income is the natron which forms at the edge of certain lakes and is still used for bread-making, tanning, and the maturing of tobacco. The natron is collected in blocks by the men, and it is customary at the beginning of the season to kill a camel beside the lake as a ritualistic sacrifice—and, of course, the opportunity of a feast. This ceremony, however, depends on whether the Dawada have a camel. I saw none in the two villages I visited. The only animals were donkeys, goats, chickens, desert rats, flies, and mosquitoes. If there should be a camel available at the beginning of the natron season, it is butchered according to the Moslem rite and allowed to bleed to death at the edge of the lake. A lot of blood is said to portend a good harvest.

Who are the Dawada, and how did they get to such a remote corner of the desert?

Without a careful anthropological study, the first of these two questions cannot be answered. All one can conclude from observing them is that they are Negroid stock, though without the markedly wide nostrils and everted lips of the central African. On the other hand, the possibility of their having Arab blood is unlikely, for the Arab invaders of the seventh and eighth centuries could not have penetrated this region. It is much more probable, therefore, that they are the last survivors of some ancient Negro race who were driven into this wilderness by invaders and have lived there ever since. A French doctor who saw them describes them as 'living fossils'.

They are not, however, primitives in the sense of the

Australian Aborigines or the Bushmen of the Kalahari Desert. To the contrary, they are a civilised, Arabic-speaking, and devoutly Moslem people who have simply been by-passed by history. There is scarcely a machine of any sort in their villages, not even a wheel—though an exception must be made for the transistor radio belonging to the headman of Mandara. I was acutely aware of this symbol of progress because it was tuned to Radio Cairo all night long, adding its interminable harangues to the non-stop crowing of the cocks.

In nearly all other respects the Dawada make do with the same implements that their forefathers used 2,000 years ago. Their houses are palm huts without any furniture whatsoever. They sleep on the ground and cook by wood fires. They draw water from the wells by baskets attached to a beam made from the trunk of a palm tree. Their miniature gardens produce a few bushels of oats. There is no industry at all and no handicrafts, other than plaiting rope from the palm fibre. They are ignorant of weaving, and the women neither sew nor knit. There are no needles to sew with, except the thorn of the *thala* bush, and no wool to card. Pottery making is also unknown, and there is no clay in any case with which to make dishes or pots.

There is no school, no doctor, no books, and nothing to do but the daily tasks necessary to stay alive. The only public activity is attendance at the mosque, which is restricted to men only. The only structure resembling a building at Gabr'aoun, the largest of the three villages, is a mosque built of blocks of natron. This place constitutes a meeting house and club for the village elders; and here they sit in rows along the wall, sometimes talking, sometimes simply staring into space.

As the women do not know how to sew or weave, the clothes of the Dawada are for the most part rags handed down from generation to generation. Some of the men who have obtained money by one means or another have a woollen burnous which the Arab uses as both a coat and a blanket. Other men have obtained an old Italian, French, or British army overcoat. The women wear black dresses, and these gloomy garments, together with their black faces, hands, and legs, tend to make them resemble bats as they flit about between their cabins at dusk. Some of the young girls wear a red cotton gown, and the more fortunate babies have little necklaces of bright beads.

The life of these 400 to 500 people, then, is the nearest thing to basic survival that can be imagined, even in an atomic age. Nature had provided just enough food to support their changeless existence. Their dates, said to be the best in Libya, are very near a complete food in themselves. The 'worms', unappetising as they may be to outsiders, provide some sort of protein. For the rest, their gardens yield a few vegetables and enough grain for an occasional loaf of bread. On high days and holidays they butcher a goat or kill a chicken. There are also eggs laid by hens not much larger than a London pigeon.

Anything else comes under the heading of luxuries and has to be obtained by barter when the annual Tuareg caravan comes through. If they have any cash the Dawada also cross the vast dunes on foot to the nearest oases outside their private desert. When they have nothing better to do they walk ten hours from one village to another. One of these excursionists accompanied our small caravan from his village of Mandara to the next settlement called Gabr'aoun. He evidently came along just for the 'ride', though he actually walked the fifteen miles non-stop through the deep sand. It was a pleasure to watch his characteristic gait—it was the proper, the only, way to walk in the desert. One marches lightly, with very short steps, sometimes trotting, and, where the sand is particularly fine and steep, digging in the toes and turning the foot as on a pivot. The Dawada can carry up to eighty pounds in this manner, running up dunes 600 feet high.

Our companion, since he was merely out for an excursion, carried nothing except his ash stick which he liked to stretch across his shoulders behind his neck as he marched along ahead of the camels. At a certain point along the route he decided to leave us. We pushed on south, he turned to the west. His village lay beyond a mountain of sand. Our farewells were brief, and the last I saw of him he was moving with short, bouncy steps up the enormous slope, a blue dot in the vast yellow desert, quite alone and quite unconcerned. Sand and solitude meant nothing to him.

I spent six days in the country of the Dawada, some of this time occupied in marching from one village to another with my small caravan, the rest living in a palm hut, walking round the lakes, and wandering through the villages.

The people were invariably friendly and hospitable and dug deep into their small stores of such luxuries as eggs and tea to entertain me, though I did my best to dissuade them and would have preferred to eat my own rations. I began to dread the unidentifiable dishes of mush that were set before me in the sand. But the laws of hospitality in the desert are inviolable: the guest must be fed, whatever the cost. The ripest dates, the choicest morsels of chicken, are personally selected for him by his host. Conversely, the guest must show appreciation and enjoyment of whatever is handed to him.

So the Dawada received me with kindness and courtesy, though I only met the men of the villages. I never spoke, of course, to the women, though I occasionally saw their faces, for they don't wear the veil, but try to cover their face with the bundle of black rags they carry about their heads. From what I saw of them, their expressions were completely impassive—with reason, for their existence is certainly more wretched than that of the men. They are condemned from childhood to the treadmill of the worm-fishing, and their hope of escape is nil.

After several days with the Dawada I began to realise what isolation could really mean. I found myself lying awake at night, listening to the thunder of some trans-continental jet flying 30,000 feet above our village in the sand sea. Lucky people!

I think the true meaning of this sort of existence was summed up for me by a man in a ragged old Italian army greatcoat who leant against the palm-tree column in my hut and expressed his thoughts in a monologue spoken in pigeon Italian. It appeared that he had spent ten years in Tripoli as a labourer, but had had to return to his village to look after his aged parents. There was nobody else to care for them. Returning, he had married and now had five children.

'There is nothing here,' he says. 'There is not even a barber. . . . Nothing. There is nothing for me to do. I look after my father and mother. My father sleeps all day. My mother is blind. We eat dates and the "worms". There is nothing else. I don't have any chickens. Some do. I don't. I had to come back—there was nobody else. . . .'

The dirge continues and repeats itself. It is the epitome of their lives.

On the sixth day I set out from Gabr'aoun, the largest of the villages (population *circa* 280). We had a march of ten hours non-stop to reach the edge of the sand sea before dark. It was a long journey. Sometimes I rode Zaila the good camel, sometimes I walked. Both modes of locomotion were to become equally painful. But, after all, I was walking away from prison. You can go a long way with that incentive.

On the last stretch we met two Dawada with their donkeys on their way back to their village. As is customary in the desert, we altered course to meet and salute them. We waved and salaam-ed and spoke cheerfully to them. They scarcely replied, scarcely looked at us at all. They passed by, their faces expressionless, going northwards into the wilderness which we were leaving, walking with the characteristic quick, short steps, prodding their donkeys ahead of them. Within a few minutes they were mere dots crawling across the immense and empty dunes. It was my last sight of the Dawada.

2 *Early Records of the 'Worm-Eaters'*

The Dawada had interested me not only as the inhabitants of a veritable lost world of Africa, but as conceivably the last survivors of a race of men who had inhabited this whole region of the Sahara Desert 5,000 years and more ago. This was the race that had made life possible in the great valleys between the limestone mountains and the sand seas. Were these aboriginal Africans the people who had built the immense hydraulic system which lay beneath these valleys, an irrigation system of hundreds of water tunnels that enabled a population far surpassing in numbers the inhabitants today to cultivate the desert? And did they develop their own system of agriculture, the discovery of which has usually been ascribed to an Aryan people from whom it spread through Egypt to the rest of Africa?

Since very few scientists from the outside world have penetrated into the Ramla el Dawada, our evidence is limited to half a dozen reports which do little to answer such questions or to solve the mystery of this 'lost' tribe. Some students see Herodotus's reference to a Libyan people 'who avoid all intercourse with other men, possess no weapons of war, and do not know how to defend themselves' as a description of this aboriginal race who fled before the invasions of white conquerors called the Garamantes.[1] Again, the Romans were certainly in this country as early as 19 B.C. when they marched through the Wadi el Ajal on a punitive campaign against the Fezzan. Whether or not the centurion of some legion climbed to the top of the first dune, and looked northwards across the Ramla el Dawada, we shall never know; but

1. Herodotus, *History*, IV, 174.

if he did he must surely have decided that such a desert was uninhabited and not worth reconnoitring. In any case, there is no mention by Roman historians of Herodotus's unsociable and defenceless Libyans. By this time the Dawada seem already to have vanished from history.

In fact their existence was not known in Europe until 1822, when, as we have seen, Oudney and Clapperton 'discovered' them. They were not seen or heard of again until thirty years later on the occasion of a flying visit by the German explorer Dr. Eduard Vogel who had been asked by the British African Society to investigate them. In order to transport his gear and scientific instruments Vogel hired five camels and set off into the sand sea. His rate of progress was less than ten miles in eighteen hours. He appears to have first reached Lake Bahar-el-Dud which Oudney and Clapperton visited; and on being told that the waters were bottomless and immediately dragged under any man who dared venture into them, the courageous German walked and swam into the lake and began taking soundings. He found its greatest depth to be around twenty-four feet. He also reported the presence of the 'worms', which he found delicious.

Either Vogel didn't actually taste them, or the proverb is right and there is no accounting for tastes. Unfortunately, the young German did not survive his African journey, for he was presumably murdered with his British servant (a soldier called MacGuire) somewhere in the desert, and his papers, meticulously written up in the highest tradition of German scholarship, were destroyed by the bandits. What we know of him and his visit to the Dawada is taken from letters which got through to the Royal Geographical Society before he died. In one of these letters he writes:

> The desert in which the lakes are found is of a horrible appearance, presenting a confusion of hills and broken valleys which form the moving sand dunes in which animals and men sink up to their chests, and where one literally doesn't find a yard of solid ground. The rate of march is just over half-a-mile an hour. One gets an idea of these moving sand hills when one

knows that one of them on the south of the Bahar-el-Dud lake is over 500 feet high . . .

There are five natron lakes (actually about a dozen including the large ponds), the deepest being 20–30 feet deep . . . The worms are extremely pretty, being bright red in colour like a dorado . . . They form the basis of a delicious 'mush'. . . .

The next to reach the lakes was Henri Duveyrier, the young French explorer who visited the 'Worm Eaters' in 1860. He, too, reports on the unusual industry of collecting 'worms' in seines from the lakes, drying them in the sun, pounding them up, and mixing them with dates to make the staple diet of the Dawada tribe. His report is more accurate than either Oudney's or Vogel's:

These worms are nothing else but the larvae of a fly to which is given the name *Arthemia oudneii*, in memory of the exploration which cost Dr. Oudney his life.

Flies and larvae are found by the million, the former on the edges of the lakes and on the water where it is dense enough to support them; the latter in recesses from which they emerge in Spring when the barley ripens and in the Autumn at the time of the date harvest. These are also the periods when the lakes are disturbed by equinoctial storms.

The bodies of these small animals are several millimeters long from head to tail, between which there runs a little intestinal canal traced out in black. The worms swim indifferently on their front or their backs.

The catch is made by means of an elongated fish net held open by a circle and pushed with a long handle.

Both the actual fishing and the preparation of the worms are a monopoly of the women.

With each catch, the worms are pounded up into briquettes and dried in the sun, then buried in sacks in the sand.

This delicacy is sold all over the Fezzan. It is eaten raw, boiled, or, more often, cooked as a sauce with a few vegetables. The taste recalls shrimps when they are getting a bit 'high'. Notwithstanding, the natives make a great thing of them.

After Henri Duveyrier's visit in 1860 the Dawada remained hidden and forgotten beside their lakes for the next seventy years or more, their only visitors from the outside world being Tuareg caravans which crossed the sand sea in order to take out the produce of the region, the worm-cakes and the blocks of natron.

So nothing more was heard of the Dawada until 1930, when the whole of Libya, including the Fezzan where they lived, became an Italian colony which the Fascist politicians announced 'must be forced to reshape itself to our methods and our will'. The handful of Italian scholars who were sent to the region were less interested in changing the aspect of the Great Desert than they were in exploring a world which had been hidden from the West since the Byzantine period. In fact almost all that we know of the history, archaeology, and anthropology of the Fezzan is based on the field work of these scholars, including Professor E. Zavattari, who finally identified the famous 'worms' of the Dawada as a crustacean called *Artemia salina* and not the larvae of some dipteral insect, as Duveyrier had thought. At the same time that the scientists were making preliminary studies of the history and ecology of the region the Italian army undertook the first census of the Fezzan, and it is from the few bald statistics of the Italian report that we obtain a simple picture of the Dawada in their wasteland of dunes.

Number of people in the three villages of Mandara, Gabr'Oun, and Trouna	286	
Number of domestic animals	28	donkeys
	1	sheep
Number of gardens	38	
ditto wells	38	
ditto date palms	6,725	

For the rest, the Italian report sums up the country of the Dawada in these words:

> There exist in all ten small lakes, blue as the sky, almost a magic vision, a promise of cool resting places in the middle of

one of the most desolate and inhospitable regions of the Sahara Desert.[1]

The explorations of the Italians during the thirties were continued by the French, who briefly occupied the Fezzan in the subsequent decade. Reading the French reports, one sometimes had the impression that the war between the soldiers of the two nations was also fought between the scholars, for a great deal of what the Italians documented is sharply criticised by the French. Certainly the latter were more thorough in their investigation of the Dawada on the occasion of their visit with a team of doctors, anthropologists, and geologists in 1949, when some light, though faint, was thrown on the history of this lost tribe.[2] The French scientists noted, for instance, that the village of Mandara boasts one of the only two solid constructions in the sand sea. The other is the mosque found in the largest of the three villages, Gabr'aoun, and is of a recent date. That at Mandara is built on a small hillock beside the lake and is made out of blocks of natron. It is, or was, obviously a fort, with the remains of a rudimentary rampart, crude bastions, and an inner citadel. Here, I was told by the villagers, were found human skeletons and, outside the fort, the bones of cattle. To this evidence of some prehistoric community who fortified their village against invaders must be added that of the German palaeontologist H. Kantner, who reported a find of Stone Age implements in the vicinity of the fort, including arrow heads.

From these slight but significant clues arises the hypothesis that the Ramla el Dawada was once a fertile region occupied by hunters, then by the herdsmen who succeeded them, and finally by a remnant of the aboriginal Negroes who were isolated behind the first dunes by the white invaders called the Garamantes.

If this supposition is correct the present-day Dawada are the last living survivors of a lost world.

1. *Il Fezzan*, Governo della Tripolitania, Ufficio Studi, No. 1, December 1932.

2. See, in particular, *Mission au Fezzan*, Institut des Hautes Études de Tunis, I 'Notes Ethnographiques', by Didier Pauphilet, pp. 113 ff., 1949.

3 *The Mystery of their Origin*

How do the Dawada survive in their wilderness?

The answer only becomes apparent after a tour of the Ramla brings a certain familiarity with the terrain itself. For, as one so often finds in the Sahara, the conditions are not as horrendous as they first appear: there is a great deal more water, for instance, than at first seems conceivable. In fact there are ten lakes of some size in the Dawada country. Nine of these lakes have two characteristics in common. They are heavily charged with carbonate of soda and other mineral salts to the degree that their water is undrinkable; and all of them maintain their level throughout the summer, despite the fact that it seldom rains sometimes for five years at a time. The lakes, then, are not dependent on local rainfall but on underground reservoirs and veins of water that maintain the watershed despite the enormous evaporation.

Moreover, the lakes, as I was frequently told by my guides, were 'bottomless', which I assumed at first meant more than a few yards deep. But they may have been right, within reason. For nobody has yet sounded the depth of all of them, since those travellers who have penetrated the Ramla and have examined the terrain have not been able to take in a boat and the necessary equipment. Some of the lakes, then—Amouna is one of them—may be extremely deep; and both the Dawada themselves as well as the Tuareg are palpably terrified of this lake, as well as the one called Oum el Hassan. Not for nothing do these desert people say that these mysterious, silent, and profoundly still pools are haunted: their legends have a basis in fact, for the dunes surrounding some of the lakes are so steep that if one started to slide down them, one would be plunged into the water below. The Tuareg can't swim, so they would expect to drown; and even a swimmer who swallowed a mouthful or two of this poisonous water would be lucky to get back to the bank; and luckier still if he could clamber out.

Yet one of the ten lakes actually contains sweet water, which indicates the presence of fresh water under the dunes. This is Lake Tademka, ten miles north-east of Gabr'aoun. This lake, however, dries up in the summer months but refills in the winter. None of the Dawada live beside this sweet-water lake for the obvious reason that it contains none of the *dood* on which they largely depend for survival. The Tuareg caravans passing through graze their camels around the banks of Tademka which is gradually being filled in with grass and reeds.

Where does all this water come from? And how is it held in the 'bowl' of the sand-dunes? The geologists[1] tell us that a huge reservoir of water lies under this region of the Sahara, trapped there from prehistoric times and partly re-supplied by rain falling in the mountain ranges and running down through crevices into the subterranean 'cisterns'. It was probably these sources of water which the builders of the *foggaras*[2] tapped in the Wadi el Ajal; and it was the knowledge that subterranean rivers or channels brought the water into the Ramla that persuaded the ancestors of the Dawada to flee into what is, to all appearances, a waterless wasteland. The most reasonable explanation is that the Ramla was habitable at the time of their migration. If they left with their cattle herds—as they must have done in order to survive—they must have known there was sufficient grazing to maintain them.

Such a hypothesis takes us back long before recorded history, which begins in this part of Africa with references in the fifth century B.C. to the presence of the Garamantes in the Fezzan. But when these white invaders actually arrived 'from across the sea' we as yet have no way of knowing. It will be argued in Book Three that they must have conquered the

1. See, in particular, Pierre Bellair, *Mission au Fezzan*, op. cit.
2. See Book Three, Chapter One.

Fezzan at a period when this region of the Sahara was relatively fertile, for it is unlikely that they would have left the coastal plains for a permanent occupation of a barren desert.

The Dawada themselves have absolutely no 'folk memory' of their origins or their history. The nearest they can get to an explanation of their ancestry is the vague myth that they are the descendants of one 'Aoun' whose tomb stands half-way up an immense sand dune outside the village of Gabr'aoun, the largest of the three settlements. The tomb consists of a truncated palm tree, surmounted by a sheep's skull. But the veneration in which sainted ancestors are usually held in Moslem countries is not apparent among the descendants of Aoun, and no Western visitor has yet been able to fathom what they actually imply by this legend. The austerity of their lives is such that they have no interest in the past or, for that matter, in the future. The days pass in a monotonous round of necessary tasks which are undertaken almost entirely by the women and children. The men's time is taken up by sitting in groups endlessly talking, or by occasional visits to one of the other two villages, though relations between the three communities are rather those of indifference than cordiality. The one unifying factor between the Dawada is their religion, for all are devout Moslems, though how and when they were converted is still another mystery, which certainly will never be solved now. One possibility is that Islam was brought to them by the Tuareg, who have been their only regular visitors from the outside world. On the other hand, the strictly orthodox version of Mohammedanism that the Dawada practise has little resemblance to the Tuareg cult, notably in the 'Worm Eaters'' attitude towards women who are segregated in the fashion of the old Moslem convention. True, the women do not wear veils, for the obvious reasons that they don't have the cotton to make these face-cloths, but they take what precautions they can to conceal themselves from a strange man's eyes by hiding their features under the rags which they wear as turbans.

The only other feasible explanation of the Dawada's adoption of Mohammedanism is that some marabout came among them in olden times, for the religious history of the desert presents many cases of such holy men retiring into the wilderness in the manner of the early Christian hermits. Perhaps the legendary Aoun was such a marabout, and the fact that the inhabitants of the Ramla still have a vague recollection of such a person suggests that he was a fairly recent arrival in their country.

Beyond this, nothing is known about their conversion, except that their religion, though strict, is characterised by various tabus and rituals which probably go back to their pagan origins. The sacrifice of a camel beside the lake at the beginning of the natron season would seem to belong to a primitive period in their culture, as do their various tabus about the lakes themselves. But no anthropologist has so far studied, let alone explained, the customs of this isolated group; and from my own experience an outsider will have difficulty in discovering anything very new or suggestive. To the Dawada, speculation about themselves is a waste of time, and their attitude is perhaps best summed up by a statement they made to a French traveller: '*Ceux qui sont morts, sont morts. Ceux qui sont partis sont partis. Car il y en a qui ont réussi à s'échapper. Ceux-là ne reviennent jamais. Ceux qui restent sont les oubliés de Dieu.*'[1]

1. 'Those who are dead are dead. Those who have left have left, because there are some who have managed to escape. They never return. Those who stay are the forgotten of God'—Philippe Diolé, *Dans le Fezzan Inconnu.* 1956, pp 54 ff.

BOOK TWO

The Rock Artists

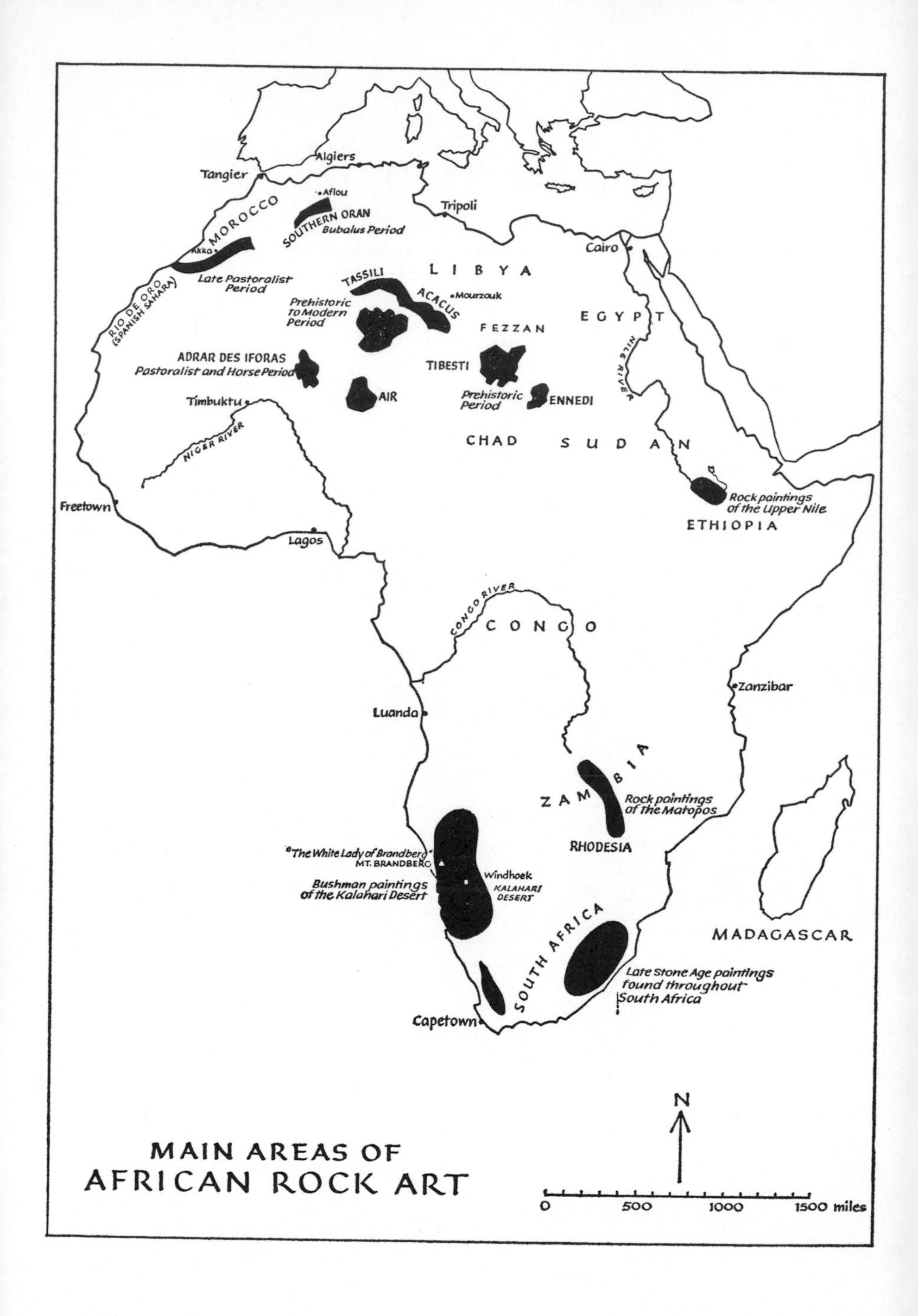

MAIN AREAS OF
AFRICAN ROCK ART

4 *Art Galleries of the Sahara*

The Acacus Mountains in south-western Libya will not be found on any but the largest-scale maps, and, apart from aerial surveys, they remain an undiscovered country to the geographers. Yet they contain one of the world's most stupendous art galleries—thousands of pictures from 10,000 B.C. upwards through time to the abandonment of what was once a sort of prehistoric African Garden of Eden.

On first seeing the Acacus range the traveller is liable to wonder if this lunar landscape is how our whole planet will look when it becomes burnt out and hence devoid of life. The black, completely eroded ridges rise in jagged masses as far as the eye can see, and there seems no way into or through them. On the outskirts of this rock mass, enormous sand-dunes reveal the ultimate process of desiccation—the Sahara Desert of popular imagination. To-day this region is the country of a few impoverished Tuareg who are probably the only people who could survive here on account of their simple camelline economy. Without a Tuareg guide, no single traveller could find his way into the Acacus, and, in any case, it is not easy to find a tribesman who knows the tracks. Perhaps these veiled men, who were once lords of the desert, prefer to retain at least one region of their old empire inviolate from Europeans. The Tuareg who eventually guided me into the mountains from the oasis of Serdeles was difficult to persuade, probably for some such reason, and at one point in our palaver simply turned away and walked back down the road to imply that negotiations were at an end.

Fortunately someone was forthcoming who could read my letters of recommendation from a Tuareg chieftain, and about midday we set off across the desert down the eastern side of the Acacus range.[1] We soon picked up the tracks of the Italian explorer Fabrizio Mori,[2] who has done for the Acacus paintings what Henri Lhote has accomplished for the Tassili-n-Ajjer in south-eastern Algeria. We followed the Mori tracks into a valley half-way down the range and by nightfall had worked our way into the centre of the massif where we made camp. After he had eaten, the Tuareg disappeared into the darkness.

He reappeared next morning, for he had not slept in our camp at all, and all indications were that somewhere in this wilderness of rock there were other tribesmen whom he had gone to visit. The presence of these Tuareg in the Acacus—there are said to be a few score of them—only added to the mystery and impression of utter loneliness that the mountains create. Thus, we never saw a human being during our stay, though as we wandered through the deep canyons which run north–south through the range, we did see the evidence of human habitation—the typical *zeribas*, or palm-thatched lean-tos of goat and camel herdsmen. Also, in the *abris*, or niches under the towering cliffs, we descried the few possessions of the little families who, however, remained completely out of sight, even if they were at the time in the region. A pot or two and a bundle of clothes were the evidence of their presence; and the coming and going of our Tuareg guide implied that he was in touch with his people. The facts are that the Acacus, like other regions of the desert which seem at first sight to be utterly abandoned, still supports life on the most primitive of levels—that is, a handful of people who know where there are small green patches of vegation and a rock pool of trapped rain water adequate to raise a few goats and feed a camel or two.

The question is why the Tuareg of the Acacus Mountains choose to live in such isolation, and the answer is a simple one. They are sustained not by food or possessions or material

1. Our expedition consisted of two R.A.F. Land Rovers of the Desert Rescue Group.

2. See Fabrizio Mori, *Tadrart Acacus*, 1965.

wealth in any form, but by a kind of pride which is as uncompromising as it is archaic. The Tuareg are the victims of their own tradition, according to which they were lords of the desert for well over a thousand years and, like the medieval barons of Europe, had no need to sow or reap or engage in business enterprises in order to prosper. Thus, their nobles were 'knights' whose sole function in life was to fight; those who fed and attended on them were serfs; and their women were the fair ladies and damsels who held courts of love not unlike those of thirteenth-century Provence.

All this seemingly elegant way of life set against the romantic background of vast desert and green oasis was only tolerable, of course, in a primitive world devoid of machines and machine-minded men. Thus, the 'charger' of the Tuareg warrior—namely, his white racing camel—and his archaic weapons, the huge leather shield with the Crusader's cross on the boss and the long lance, were little better as fighting tools than prehistoric man's bows and arrows, once the rifle and the machine-gun arrived in the desert. Moreover, both the trade and the control of the caravan routes which were a monopoly of the Tuareg were supervised and administered by Europeans following the conquest of North Africa. The trans-Saharan slave trade was put a stop to; the other commodities, like salt, formerly carried across the desert on the backs of thousands of camels bred by the Tuareg, were now transported in diesel trucks.

Yet the Tuareg stubbornly refused to compromise with modernity in any shape or form; and so one finds them in regions like the Acacus or the Tassili-n-Ajjer or the Hoggar Mountains reduced to the lowest level of existence. Their traditional scorn of urbanisation inhibits them from living in towns, or even houses, which they regard as a sign of decadence. In fact, they so despise the refinements of civilisation that they would rather go hungry than become servants of any kind. They often refuse to send their children to school, or to take advantage of Western services like hospitals and clinics. They are, in short, the last of those 'noble savages' the philosophers have extolled from their armchairs without ever having personally experienced the privations of primitive life.

In the Acacus Mountains, then, the struggle for bare survival is one which civilised men can scarcely envisage. Dirt, disease, and near starvation are the everyday facts of existence. One meal a day consisting of a few dates and a little goats' milk is about all the Tuareg nomads can expect. The children will spend hours waiting at a lizard's hole in the hope of catching a mouthful or two of 'meat'. The extreme heat does not bother them, but they suffer terribly from the cold on winter nights, for few of them can afford a woollen blanket and must live and sleep in their thin cotton robes, which, like their bodies, are never washed.

Yet, to the Tuareg the hunger, cold, and privations have compensations. They are the price of solitude and the knowledge that a man is his own master—the proof that to be a Tuareg is to be superior to all the townsmen, tradesmen, and wage-earners in the world. This attitude, or philosophy even, explains why there are still a few score of people inhabiting the eroded and infertile country to which we had to bring every single necessity, including water. It also explains why our guide was completely at home in the mountains, disappearing for long periods down the ravines or over the bare rocks, as if indifferent to the food and shelter of our camp: he obviously preferred the company of his own people, and, for all one knew, had a little *pied-à-terre* of his own here in the wilderness —a wife, children, a straw hut, and a few goats. I could not ask him the answer to these questions, for he only spoke *temajegh*, the verbal language of the Tuareg. Conversation between us was therefore impossible.

Such is Acacus and the other Saharan art galleries today, a lost world of crumbling cliffs, sand-clogged valleys, and occasional tufts of camel grass, a silent world haunted by the ghosts of a race of men who might have come from another planet, so far away in time and space are they from life as we know it today. One looks up at some mountain crest and is convinced that there is one of their castles atop it, complete with towers, bastions, and crenellated walls. Great pillars and domes abound on all sides, not sculpted by man, but by nature, for the physical forces in this region of the Sahara are absolutely relentless: the rocks are continuously being blasted into dust by wind and sand, the sun bakes them by day, the frosts shatter them by night.

Here 10,000 years ago lived a race of hunters together with thousands of animals great and small now only found in the rivers and jungles of Central Africa. Along these rock-enclosed corridors between the cliffs marched herds of elephants, giraffes, and buffalo. Baboons swung from the branches of trees; lions hunted the gazelles; and rhinoceroses charged through the undergrowth. All these animals came down to the rivers and lakes to drink wary of each other and especially of the crocodiles that lay with the snouts and eyes just above water. By preying on each other, all found enough to eat; and chief of the predators was a numerous race of men who hunted with throwing sticks, bows and arrows, and long spears.

It was these men, the black contemporaries of their white brothers to the north in the caves and forests of southern Europe, who left us a strangely compelling picture of their world.

The story they tell begins with the depiction on the rock faces of the big game they hunted—elephants, lions, giraffe, moufflon, wild boar, and even aquatic animals like hippopotamuses. Thousands of such pictures line the sides of the now-deserted wadis, making a frieze on the cliffs for hundreds of yards in length. The Acacus Mountains 8,000 to 10,000 years ago, therefore, must have been forested, and the desolate valleys watered by rivers. The denizens of these forests and prairies dwelt under the sharp eyes of the cliff-dwellers who stalked them by day and drew them in the summer evenings. The Sahara Desert at that time was an actual version of an African Garden of Eden.

The traveller to the Acacus, or any of the other great art galleries of the Sahara, can catch a glimpse of that almost mythical world since there is nothing between him and these prehistoric artists to prevent the transition in imagination through ten millennia of time. There is not, for instance, a vestige of the modern world in these desert wildernesses, long since abandoned by all except a few invisible nomads. The cliffs, rocks, and wadis remain as they were when the last of the primitive men abandoned them. And thus, standing in the valleys between the cliffs, the traveller can look up and see that lost world in the form of a procession of fantastic creatures engraved for all time on the sometimes inaccessible rock faces. Most of the animals are now only familiar to us from zoos or wild-game reserves; many are becoming increasingly rare even in Africa. The elephant is here, exactly as some artist saw him 10,000 years or more ago, and exactly as he is today, for in the oldest and best engravings he is reproduced with meticulous attention to detail—the small, shrewd eyes, huge, flapping ears, sinuous trunk, and massive feet. So, too, the larger and fiercer animals are invariably the most realistically drawn, as if they presented the greatest threat to the hunter armed with his stone axe or tiny bow. The hippopotamuses, rhinoceroses, giraffes, lions, and panthers are all caught in characteristic attitudes, lumbering along, or towering above us with their long necks, or crouched ready to spring. In fact there is hardly an African animal that is not represented, including one which is extinct, the *Bubalus antiquus*, or prehistoric buffalo, as well as aquatic species whose presence on the rock faces proves beyond doubt that the Great Desert, 10,000 years ago, had its lakes and marshes as well as rivers and forests. The ancient Saharans must, therefore, have spent many a long day crouched in the reeds observing the comings and goings of these water animals, the crocodile waiting just below the surface of a lake, the pelican fishing at the verge. It is significant that where man himself is portrayed he is shown as a small, crouching figure armed with his throwing-stick, axe, or bow and, in one picture, dead at the feet of an elephant.

The oldest pictures, then, are engravings of wild beasts found high up on cliff faces, and they were the first to be seen by white travellers. The discovery of the wall paintings found in niches or under overhanging rocks where prehistoric men sheltered from the sun and rain (for there are very few actual caves in the Sahara) came later. It is still not known whether the paintings are as old as the oldest engravings which can be roughly dated to 10,000 B.C., though we know from the examples of European rock art that wall paintings were being executed as long ago as 40,000 B.C. It has been suggested that prehistoric men made the engravings, women the paintings—a theory that is not likely ever to be proved or disproved. The supposition appears to be that men occupied themselves sculpting the rock faces of the cliffs. Perhaps the theory should not be too summarily dismissed, since the African paintings reveal a new and different world from the engravings—a more social and even domestic world in which women are introduced for the first time in prehistoric art. Thus, outside on the bare cliffs, we have a typically masculine view of life as a continual warfare between the hunter and his prey; inside, in the rock shelters, small and intimate depictions of social activities. This 'interior' world is more humanised and more familiar. Leisure and entertainment are now facets of existence, even at this level. Music, dancing, and perhaps even games were a feature of communal life as the culture evolved from a hunting to a pastoral society. Women now appear in their primitive finery and are even shown beautifying themselves, nursing their children, or engaged in household chores. They are depicted as taking part in certain rites, though the significance of these so-called religious scenes is still a matter of speculation. After all, it is little more than a hundred years since the existence of prehistoric art has been known; and less than fifty years since systematic studies of it have been undertaken. Even now we cannot say with certainty who actually made these pictures, let alone why. For while work on the European cave paintings has been intensive, and many problems, notably that of dating, have been largely solved, the whole subject of African art remains extremely controversial, to the extent that the basic questions still remain unanswered. Were the North African engravings, for instance, the work of a white or a Negro race? Is there a connection between the painters of the South European school and those of North and South Africa? How were the rocks actually incised? And what was the purpose of the pictures—magical, ritualistic, or recreational? And what do the engravings, apart from the simple portraits of hunting or cattle-herding, actually mean?

As the literature on the subject grows larger, the answers to these questions seem to grow less convincing. Even in the matter of time, there is no firm agreement. Thus, we have instances of cave paintings whose dating varies by as much as 3,000 years, and one famous example of Bushman art ascribed to 1500 B.C. by one school of experts and to A.D. 1800 by another.[1]

1. The example is 'The White Lady of Brandberg', a Bushman painting discovered in 1917 by a German prospector in the Brandberg Mountains of South West Africa. The Abbé Breuil, most famous and revered of Rock Art specialists, tentatively subscribed to the theory that the 'White Lady' was Cretan and, if so, that she was painted as early as 1500 B.C. by a Greek artist. Some South African students, on the other hand, prefer the theory that she is a Bushman portrait of a white woman missionary, in which case she dates from the nineteenth century A.D.

5 *'Lascivious Pictures . . .'*

The deep significance of prehistoric art, both that found in the European caves and that on the African cliff sides, was at first dismissed by scholars on the grounds that 'cavemen' were incapable of that degree of cultural awareness needed to produce works of such a high aesthetic order. Primitive man was supposed to be an ape-like creature whose only artifacts were tools and weapons of stone. He was thought to be devoid of the principal attributes of mind and spirit which differentiate man as we know him from the brute creation. Hence the response of the scholars to the cave paintings of Altamira in Spain when they were first announced to the world in 1879 was really not surprising: they were dismissed as forgeries at the Lisbon conference of the Congress of Anthropology and Prehistoric Archaeology in 1880. Fifteen years later the pronouncement of the French palaeontologist Cartailhac that the Spanish cave paintings were truly great works of art was received with scepticism by some of his fellow workers and with derision by others. The fact of the matter was that European scholars, steeped in the Greco-Roman tradition, were convinced that prehistoric man, whether he belonged to the white or black race, could not conceivably have produced paintings of such skill that they actually incorporated a knowledge of the laws of perspective, a technique which was not properly understood and applied until the Italian Renaissance.

The response to the discovery of the prehistoric African rock art was even more confused, for here there was no suggestion of fraud, as there had been with the Altamira pictures. In point of time, that discovery was made before the

European cave art was known, or even suspected. The first African travellers to the Dark Continent had, in fact, frequently mentioned the engravings of cattle and human figures with animal heads; and Heinrich Barth in his thorough way made sketches of some of them which he brought back to Europe for examination by the experts in 1855. The palaeontologists gave their verdict that the African pictures were the work of the Carthaginians.

But even before Barth drew attention to the existence in the Sahara Desert of these strange drawings, other finds had been made by French army officers in Algeria as early as 1847. In the course of a punitive expedition against the Berbers of the Atlas Mountains Dr. Felix Jacquot, assistant medical officer to the Fifth Regiment of Tirailleurs, and Captain Koch of the Foreign Legion came across one of the African art galleries and reported their findings to Paris.

> These remarkable images [Dr. Jacquot writes] are engraved on the rock and portray, in the most gross and primitive manner, a number of hunting scenes, as well as scenes of the most frightful obscenity . . . These lascivious pictures will never issue from our sketch-book.[1]

It might be noted that moral indignation comes oddly from the pen of Dr. Jacquot, since elsewhere in his account of General Cavaignac's expedition against the Berbers he justifies the looting and pillaging permitted the French soldiers as a compensation for their boredom during the campaign. '*Le sac et le pillage*', he writes. '*Qui aurait la cruauté et l'injustice de lui en faire un crime?*' But as far as the 'lascivious pictures' were concerned, he compromises with his conscience by refusing to reproduce them graphically while giving a verbal description in some detail. This is how he reports his historic find:

> One sees here, without veils or mystery, that commerce against nature which brought fire and brimstone on those cities whose

1. Dr. Felix Jacquot, *Expédition du General Cavaignac dans le Sahara algérien*, 1849, pp. 149 ff.

names you know—the disgusting union which was, incidentally, far from unknown among the Romans, since their poets celebrate it in their pastorals:

> Formosum pastor Corydon ardebat Alexin,
> Delicias domini; nec, quid speraret, habebat.

> And that strange perversion which, according to Theocritus, enamoured the Sicilian shepherds of their goats, also has its counterpart at Thiout; only the rustic animal is here replaced by a lion. The result of these strange amours is revealed inside the body of the lion: it is an antelope.[1]

Dr. Jacquot, it turns out, was shocked unnecessarily, since he misinterpreted what he saw. The creature which he imagined was the offspring of the man and the lion is the drawing of a bull superimposed on the earlier engraving. In short, the various animals composing the montage were not the work of a single artist and have no connection with each other, for we know now that the initial engravings are often overlaid with later pictures, and this is the explanation of Dr. Jacquot's hybrids.

Yet we are not entitled to feel superior to the young French doctor who was the first modern European to gaze on these scenes from a world that was lost in the mists of prehistory. In fact, what Dr. Jacquot was attempting in his description of the Thiout engravings was what the experts and specialists on rock art have continued to do ever since: namely, to interpret the mind and intention of primitive men by the psychological and moral standards of the twentieth century. The result has been that prudish observers have condemned as obscene those pictures in which sex is represented either realistically or symbolically; or, alternatively, have attempted to explain them away by references to 'fertility rites' and 'ritual magic'.

Two examples of this subjective interpretation of African rock art will suffice to show the degree of guesswork that is still the basis of this branch of scholarship. One is a rock painting found in Southern Rhodesia. This highly stylised and vivid picture shows a man lying on his back. He appears to be

1. *op. cit.* p. 149.

wearing some kind of mask and is covered either with a blanket or his garment. He is surrounded by smaller figures, two of which have well-defined penises. The sex of the others is uncertain. But one thing is very certain. The man on his back is having an orgasm: thus, his organ is enlarged and erect and his semen is shown spurting upwards and curving outwards to where it makes a blob on the ground. Nothing could be more pictorially obvious than this. Yet how do the experts interpret this scene?

'Burial scene,' says Professor Leo Frobenius. 'A lying figure (dead king?) wearing a mask; below it a smaller lying figure, also accompanying figures, probably priests.'[1]

Such an interpretation is surely untenable, for whatever the supine figure is, he certainly isn't dead, and, from the look of him, is in no mood to be buried. But if the viewer denudes his mind of the 'scientific' terminology, and allows his eyes to interpret the scene, he soon perceives that the recumbent man is having an erotic dream, for in addition to his orgasm, we see what is manifestly his dream-vision in the form of a woman lying with her knees up and her legs apart in the coitus position. The woman is placed just below his head, as if having issued from his dream-thoughts.

The method, then, of judging an unknown culture by our own moral and religious values is liable to add to the bewilderment, and sometimes the confusion, which at present characterise the field of prehistoric art; and the particular examples which have just been discussed illustrate how this may occur. There are others. We find in Africa paintings of a person or persons, always women, in what the experts call the *orante*, or praying, attitude: that is, figures apparently standing with their arms bent at the elbow and their hands raised on either side of their face, almost precisely in the posture of early Christians at prayer. This posture, whose significance is unmistakable in the case of early Christian paintings, is apparently also found drawn on rocks in many parts of the world—in Australia, for example, where it is the work of the Aborigines; and in

1. Leo Frobenius and Douglas C. Fox, *Prehistoric Rock Pictures in Europe and Africa*, The Museum of Modern Art, New York, 1937.

Africa where it was the work of prehistoric artists. On the basis of this seeming resemblance, some observers have gone so far as to interpret the rock drawings in the light of the Christian paintings, as though the figures in the former were engaged in the act of worship, somewhat in the manner of the first Christians taking part in the sacrament of the Eucharist.

But what is the more realistic interpretation? The interested student must examine for himself these pagan representations of 'praying women' and draw his own conclusions. The famous fresco of Sefar found in the Tassili-n-Ajjer in south-eastern Algeria (the prehistoric art gallery which is almost contiguous to the one in the Libyan Acacus) is perhaps the best example. Henri Lhote, its discoverer, has described it as 'The Great God with Praying Women'.[1] But what do we see if we regard this picture without preconceived theories of its religious or magical significance? First, the 'Great God' himself obviously has a symbolically exaggerated organ hanging down between his legs, together with what appear to be bulging muscles on his shoulders, presumably indicative of immense virility, while the surrounding women are depicted with grossly enlarged sex characteristics. Several of these women, in fact, are shown in the coitus position, lying on their backs with their legs apart. The question is, does this scene represent a religious or 'fertility' rite? Or does it portray in simple, frank terms primitive man's dream of sexual indulgence?

To answer this question, it is helpful to ask the opinion of those nearest in mentality to the original artists. I tried this approach on my Tuareg guide in the Acacus Mountains, showing him the portrait of a woman in the supposedly *orante* attitude; but he was not to be drawn. But the manner in which he turned away with a 'closed face', as though implying the subject was distasteful, suggested its own answer. Indeed, the answer was considerably more revealing in the case of the Australian Aborigines who, when shown a painting of a 'praying woman' (that is, with arms raised), laughed contemptuously at their ancestors' picture and stated categorically

1. Henri Lhote, *The Search for the Tassili Frescoes*, 1959.

that it was the portrait of a 'she-devil, because she-devils always *lie down* in this indecent posture'.[1] In other words, what the European observer might convince himself is a quasi-religious picture, with spiritual undertones, may be simply the very down-to-earth primitive version of sexual intercourse. What is decisive, of course, is the prehistoric artist's obvious inability to solve the technical problem of depicting a figure in a foreshortened supine position. The best he could do was to draw the figure with the arms raised and the legs apart, though he failed to make his subject appear to be lying down in this attitude.

The inconclusive character of certain academic interpretations of prehistoric art, then, inclines the observer to question many of the explanations which now tend to be automatically accepted and to view the records of the rocks as the expression of primitive man's need for information, recreation, and entertainment. Such a view presupposes that our ancestors were not the 'cavemen' of popular tradition: that is, they needed, in addition to food and shelter, the compensations of a social and intellectual life, however unsophisticated that life may have been. They enjoyed, no doubt, the pleasures of story-telling, which some excelled in verbally, others pictorially. The hundreds of thousands of rock pictures all over Africa, moreover, suggest that the rock faces of the cliffs and the walls of the shelters served as 'newspapers' to their prehistoric viewers, as they continue, for that matter, to do to this day; for innumerable scenes obviously portray important events in the life of the community. Sometimes they depict the arrival in the neighbourhood of strangers whose costume and arms were more easily described by means of a sketch than by words. This, at least, is the impression one gets squatting in an *abri* examining the more striking figures painted on the rock walls; and one finds oneself asking, for instance, if two miniature figures side by side, each in a helmet, cloak, and leggings, could not be some first-century B.C. artist's impression of the Roman legionnaires who marched through the Fezzan

1. Agnes Susanne Schulz, 'North-west Australian Rock Paintings'. *Memoirs of the National Museum of Victoria*, No. 20. 1956.

at this important period in Saharan history. There is no doubting the message in the case of the extraordinary drawings of the Garamantes' four-horse chariots, of which Herodotus spoke in his account of Africa, though whether these depictions were made by the Garamantes themselves as signposts of their chariot routes across the Sahara, or whether they were drawn by the Negro aborigines to warn their fellows of the new war machine, is a matter of conjecture. But the majority of the pictures do seem to be straightforward illustrations of daily life; hence the overall impression is that they represent primitive man's principal means of communication rather than the evidence of his preoccupation with the mysteries of existence.

This is not to say that these old hunters and herdsmen were devoid of the spiritual attributes which distinguish men from brute creation, especially if we include the capacity to appreciate the beauty and terror of the world around as a manifestation of such attributes. For it is clear that once the primitive African had taken the long step in evolution from killing animals for food to rearing them, he was able to live in greater security; and security gave him greater leisure. He used this leisure time making pendants of pretty stones, or armlets of schist, and necklaces of ostrich shells for his women, or decorating the rock walls of his shelter beneath the overhanging cliffs. In fact, the astonishingly keen sense of observation, technical skill, and decorative sense of these prehistoric artists entitle them to be ranked among the great naturalistic painters of history. In comparison with their pastoral scenes, the Roman and Byzantine productions, whether executed in mosaic or painted with coloured wax on wood, strike us as quite archaic, what with their stylised features and lack of emotion. By the same token, a great deal of ancient art has this vaguely inhuman quality which reaches its culmination in Egyptian portraits, Easter Island statues, and the Central African masks. The two exceptions to this general rule are Greek sculpture and prehistoric rock drawings, both of which were concerned not with ritual, but with reality. It could, therefore, be argued that the Greek sculptor and the

Stone Age painter held the opposite view of the Platonic Doctrine of Forms, whereby the realm of sensible appearance is considered wholly unreal. To them this realm was not only essentially real; it was the only one which was true.

But whereas the rock artists of the first period seemed to have had no difficulties in producing pictures of this high naturalistic order (despite their lack of tools), their successors gradually lost some of their predecessors' skill and inspiration, for we find the later engravings more stylised, which is much the same as saying less skilfully drawn. This process of making do with rough outlines for the sure, clean line of the first artists continues through successive ages until we reach the modern doodlings of passing Tuareg tribesmen, and these have no aesthetic value or interest at all. So we can almost date rock art by the artistic quality of successive periods, as well as by subject matter, and thus arrive at the following main categories on which most students are now agreed:

I. The Hunters (*circa* B.C. 10,000–B.C. 5000)
II. The Cattle Herders (B.C. 5000–B.C. 2000)
III. The Garamantian Invasion (B.C. 2000–A.D. 200)
IV. The Camel Period (A.D. 200–A.D. 1000)
V. The Modern Period

6 *The Message of Stone Age Art*

When we come to the delineations of the human face and figure we find that the rock artists, however skilful they were at depicting animals, seem never to have acquired the knack of portraiture as we know it. It is possible that here we are in the realm of the tabu, though in view of the number of attempts to show both men and women in various poses it is more likely that a lack of technique is involved. There were occasional artists of genius who captured their human subjects in motion, and we have many brilliant pictures of men running. More rare are figures in repose. The general practice seems to have been that followed by very young children when faced with the same problem of drawing a 'man'. The oldest representations, in fact, are almost precisely of this order where the figure has a blob for a head, an ellipse for the body, and stick-like appendages representing arms and legs. Later representations take the form of ghost-like, round-headed creatures without recognisable features, again reminiscent of the work of very young children. This formula seems to have been replaced by a more stylised version executed by means of two inverted and contingent triangles, often with a decapitated neck stump, or a tiny head in the shape of a dot. None of these depictions tell us how the subjects actually looked, though the experts make what they can of such clues as suggested by recognisable physical characteristics, like the elongated legs and protuberant buttocks of certain Negro races. Others discern in the portraits the faces, head-dresses, or ornaments of Libyan, Semitic, or Egyptian people.

In general, the artists seem unconscious of race or colour, and restrict themselves to depicting, as best they can, the daily activities of their male subjects and the desirability of the females. The latter are usually plump, which is to be expected, since obesity has always been the African ideal of beauty in women. Even the Stone Age statuettes of the so-called Venuses are of this order, the most famous of them, the Willendorf Venus, reminding us of those unfortunate girls the early African travellers saw being fattened up in huts until they became so adipose that they could not stand up at all. Until we have other evidence that the sculptor who fashioned these statuettes, or the men who gazed on them, were inspired with religious fervour, there are no grounds for asserting that these ancient Venuses, whether moulded in clay or drawn on the rocks, were objects of veneration. To the contrary, the crudity with which many of these artifacts emphasise an obvious sexual *motif* seems to preclude the interpretation that they symbolise fertility rites or the cult of maternity.[1] It is true that nearly all the palaeolithic Venuses accentuate the three erotic zones—breasts, pudenda, and buttocks—to a point where the limbs (head, arms, feet) are either non-existent, or merely shadowed in, as in the case of vestigial arms resting on enormous breasts. Yet, significantly, not one of the Venuses is shown with an infant (as the Madonna is conventionally portrayed) and not one of them has the aura we associate with motherhood.

It is difficult, then, to accept without reservations the theory that Stone Age art was inspired by religious motives. In the first place, there is too much of it, implying that picture-making was a folk pastime and that the rock engravings were simply the 'books' of the community. To see these pictures *in situ* gives precisely that impression: anybody who felt like it obviously tried his hand at drawing or painting, either to amuse himself and his viewers or, in some cases, to convey important new information. When a people has no written language at all and only a limited vocabulary (the Bushmen and Australian Aborigines are living examples) they have to use pictures in order to communicate. The African art galleries are full of such 'communiqués', and we may be sure that such

1. See, for instance, Paolo Graziosi, *Palaeolothic Art*, 1960, p. 57.

important events in the lives of the native Saharans as the arrival of the Garamantes with their four-horse chariots were depicted in this way. One glance at the oldest (and best) of these drawings conveys the idea of the appearance, construction, team, and especially the speed of such a vehicle—the horses at a 'flying gallop' and the driver leaning almost horizontally forward as though to emphasise the tremendous speed of the chariot. The whole contrivance must have seemed phenomenal to the Negro pastoralists who had never gone faster than they could run or an ox could carry them. They had probably seen neither a horse nor a wheel when the news came through that a warlike people had arrived in this manner from the north.

The need to convey information, then, must have been one reason for the rock pictures; the need for relaxation and amusement another. What else was there to do in the caves of southern Europe, for instance, during the long winter days and nights apart from discussing the size, ferocity, and vulnerability of animals? So in the shelters under overhanging cliffs in the Sahara Desert and on the mountainsides elsewhere in Africa, families and tribes who were well supplied with food after the day's hunt had many hours to while away, and what would be more natural than for a man to pick up a nearby flint and to amuse himself seeing if he could depict the animal he had stalked and perhaps killed that morning? In fact, judging from the mere size of some of the engravings—a rhinoceros found in a wadi south of the Mourzouk Sand Sea measures over fourteen feet in length—the artists may have worked as a group. There are, indeed, so many pictures of varying degrees of skill that obviously 'rock painting' was the favourite pastime of prehistoric man, filling his leisure hours, satisfying his need for entertainment, and expressing his desires. In brief, all his intellectual and artistic powers were canalised into this one outlet for several thousand years.

This ancient custom of using the rocks as 'newspapers' continued, in fact, up to that period when the aboriginal ways of life were affected by the civilised world outside. It certainly continued, in a debased form, throughout the great days of the caravans when travellers used the rocks to record their passing either in pictures scratched on the smooth surfaces or in writing carved on fallen stones. The caravan stopped for the night at the base of a cliff. The men hobbled their camels, lit their fire, ate their meal of dates, and brewed their tea in little cheap pots. Some gossiped, some wrapped themselves in their blanket, and some religious-minded traveller would start inscribing a *sura* from the Koran on the rock face against which he rested; or, if he had been to Mecca by sea, he might attempt a sketch of a steamboat which his companions had neither seen nor, for that matter, could imagine.

Yet there is an immense difference between the *graffiti* executed since the beginning of the Christian era and those pictures engraved or painted before it. We have already pointed out that the major difference is, in principle, the artistic superiority of the older works. A second difference is one of actual size, since the earlier artists almost invariably worked on a large 'canvas', often high on the side of an exposed cliff; the later on small, smooth surfaces found under overhanging ledges. The earliest engravings must have taken a long time to complete, whereas nearly all the recent pictures give the impression of having been drawn *en passant*. A third difference is that the oldest, and best, examples of rock art are usually found in the most inaccessible regions of the desert.

It is the combination of these factors—quality, size, and remoteness—which gives the traveller to the great art galleries like the Acacus, the Tassili-n-Ajjer, the Mourzouk Sand Sea, and the Tibesti the impression that he is looking at a lost world, and, in a very real sense, he is. For there are few places elsewhere on our planet where life has undergone such a profound change—from lush forest to barren desert. Hence it is that the representations of the huge animals on the sides of the ravines evoke the same sense of wonder that we experience in the presence of the other monuments of antiquity. And whether we subscribe to the theory that these art galleries were the temples of prehistory or not, we must recognise that man's artistic awakening began much farther back in time than we are led to believe from a perusal of the usual Stone Age artifacts. For flints, arrow heads, and stone axes do not tell us very much about the mind or spirit of primitive man. His pictures speak to us in a language we understand and tell us what the world looked like in the morning of history.

BOOK THREE

The People of the Chariots

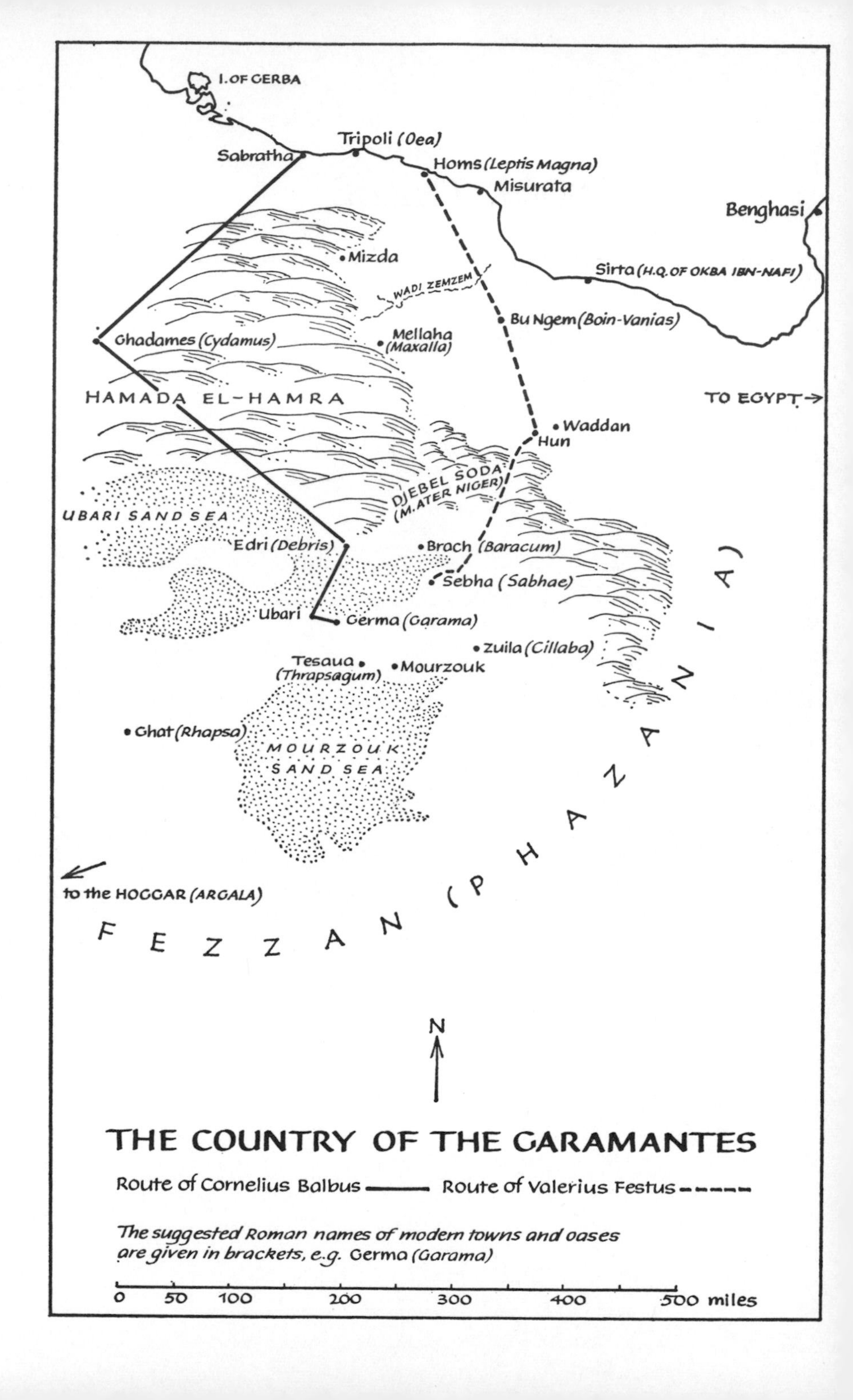

THE COUNTRY OF THE GARAMANTES

Route of Cornelius Balbus ——— Route of Valerius Festus - - - - -

The suggested Roman names of modern towns and oases are given in brackets, e.g. Germa (Garama)

7 *The Water Tunnels*

On the track which runs across the desert from Sebha, the modern capital of the Fezzan, to the oasis of Ghat on the Algerian border, the traveller crosses an underground water system that has few parallels for ingenuity and effort in African history. The system, consisting of a series of parallel and interconnecting shafts called *foggaras*, seems to have been the work of the descendants of the same race whom we first met as the hunters and artists of the Acacus Mountains.

Little, if anything, is known about these *foggaras* which, while they resemble the irrigation tunnels of Persia, are basically different in construction. The Persian tunnels, or *qanats*, as they are called, are still in use, and are characterised by having manholes at regular intervals. The Saharan *foggaras* were apparently either driven through the rock under the desert floor, or were dug out as canals and then roofed over. One finds places here and there in the Fezzan system where the roof has caved in, and one opening is pointed out as the spot where a tunnel collapsed, burying a French explorer alive. The report is probably exaggerated, but it is characteristic of the local attitude towards the ancient monuments of the region, all of which tend to become associated with the malevolent spirits of Moslem legend. The traveller who is indifferent to these djinn can descend into a *foggara* and so obtain the best impression of their size and construction.

But first, viewed from a height, the system is seen to comprise a series of embankments which run in a straight line from the base of the cliffs in the south across the sandy plain to the oases in the north. Seen from inside, the main tunnels are at least ten feet high and twelve feet wide and have been hacked out of the limestone rock by rough tools, with no attempt to smooth the surface of the roof and walls. On either side of the tunnel, latitudinal shafts branch off so as to connect with the main *foggaras*. How many of them actually remain is still not certain, though hundreds of them are still visible. In places they run less than twenty feet apart and their average length, from the cliffs where they originate to the oases where they terminate, is three miles. If we assume from the 230 that remain visible that there may have been as many as 300 of them in this region of the desert, we have, taking into account the lateral shafts, nearly 1,000 miles of tunnels hewn out of the rock under the desert floor.

We are still not clear as to how the system worked. First, where is the entrance to these tunnels? One can spend hours trying to find their inlet, and though the solution would seem easy at first, assuming that a particular mound is followed along its entire length, the investigator finally arrives at a jumble of rocks at the base of the escarpment without being able to tell where the tunnel has disappeared to. The question, therefore, is: did the builders drive their shafts right into the rock to tap underground springs? Or did they make artificial reservoirs at the end of the tunnels, these reservoirs, or pools, feeding the system with the rain water which ran down the gullies of the cliffs?

There seems to be some evidence for the latter theory, since there are signs that these gullies and ravines have been dammed with barrages of stones roughly cemented with clay. On the other hand, this method of capturing water presupposes an adequate and regular rainfall, in which case we have to go back possibly as far as 3000 B.C. to find such a maritime climate in the Sahara Desert. Could the *foggaras* be that old?

We do not know for sure, but it seems much more likely that the tunnels were built because there was *not* sufficient rainfall and hence they must have been driven right into the escarpment in order to tap underground springs. So far, no one has been able to prove or disprove either hypothesis, since the source of the water which, in a few cases, still trickles through the *foggaras* is not known. However, those geologists who have studied the region are of the opinion that veins of water, fed by the rains on far distant mountains, are the explanation of this particular system of hydraulics.[1]

In the absence of conclusive geological or archaeological evidence we can only make certain assumptions concerning the *foggaras*. First, the fact that there are so many of them indicates the presence of a numerous population which needed far more water than could be supplied by wells. Wells are the only water sources in the Wadi el Ajal today, and they are adequate for the present population of some 7,000 people. If we compare this figure with the 100,000 or more graves so far found in the Wadi and dating from the time of the 'people of the water tunnels', we can get some idea of how populous this region was and why so many irrigation tunnels were necessary. They were necessary not only for human needs but for the flocks and herds which required large tracts of pasture land, if the inhabitants of the region were still raising beef cattle; and also for the fields and gardens which supplied the population with grain and vegetables. In other words, the race which had formerly existed as hunters, living on the flesh of wild animals and the roots of wild plants, had now developed a system of agriculture without which a large settled community is impossible. In addition, the construction of such an enormous hydraulic complex indicates an industrious and technologically advanced people who had reached a stage of culture superior to that of northern Europe before the Roman conquest.

We can, therefore, safely assume that (a) between 5000 and 1000 B.C. a cattle-raising and agricultural people belonging to the Negro race had occupied large areas of the Sahara Desert which they kept habitable and fertile by means of the *foggaras*; and (b) it was precisely the prosperity of these defenceless Africans that incited the white settlers along the Libyan coast to invade the Fezzan. These immigrants (originally, it seems, having come to Africa from Asia Minor) were the Garamantes,

1. See, in particular, Pierre Bellair, *Contribution à l'Étude de l'Hydro géologie de la Cuvette Fezzanaise* (Mission Scientifique du Fezzan, 1944–5).

the people of the four-horse chariots—first mentioned by Herodotus, who describes them as already a very great nation in his time. They thereupon appear and disappear throughout the classical period until, around A.D. 700, they vanish altogether as the last of their kings was led away to captivity by the Arab invaders of the Fezzan. Their Saharan empire had lasted over a thousand years.

Yet we know almost next to nothing about the Garamantes, and the reason is obvious: with the fall of the Roman Empire, Africa became a 'lost' continent, so much so that no European traveller reached even as far south as the Fezzan until the beginning of the nineteenth century. One of the first to do so was the same Dr. Walter Oudney who discovered the Dawada; and it was this young explorer who drew the attention of the European historians to the existence of an unmistakably Roman monument at an oasis called Germa. Germa, a miserably poor village in Oudney's day and now abandoned altogether, was rightly assumed to be the same as Garama, the capital of the Garamantes; and the presence of a Roman tomb nearby attested to the conquest of the Garamantian Empire by the legions in 19 B.C., as the historian Pliny has recorded. In fact, Pliny lists the fourteen cities which the Roman General Cornelius Balbus captured, and some of these places have been definitely identified (Cydamus=Ghadames; Garama=Germa); some tentatively so (Rapsa=Ghat; Cillaba=Zuila); and others not at all. For his victory over the Garamantes and his conquest of the Fezzan, Balbus was given a triumph on his return to Rome, the first foreigner (he was a Spaniard of Cadiz) ever to be so honoured. Thereafter the Garamantes and their capital Garama were as familiar names to an informed Roman as were the Britons and their capital London. The Garamantes, however, were not occupied militarily, for the Caesars realised that no army could effectively control an area as vast as the Central Sahara. Instead, the Romans made an alliance with the native kings which lasted, despite occasional revolts, for over 500 years.

This alliance was necessary because the Garamantes, as masters of the desert, controlled the caravans that came up from Central Africa to the ports along the south Mediterranean coast. The trans-Saharan trade consisted of ivory, gold dust, ostrich feathers, animal skins, slaves, and wild animals. The importance of the last item cannot be underestimated, for wild animals were slaughtered by the thousands in the amphitheatres of the Roman world, and Africa was the chief source of supply.

Some idea of the number and type of wild beasts used in the games at Rome alone is seen from the statistics given by Roman historians. In 55 B.C. Pompey celebrated his victories by turning loose 600 lions in the arena during the five days devoted to the *venatio*: that is, simulated hunting in the amphitheatre. In A.D. 81 the Emperor Titus presented 9,000 animals; twenty-five years later Trajan raised this total to 11,000. In A.D. 248 the Emperor Philip, an Arab by birth and (according to Gibbon) 'consequently, in the earlier part of his life, a robber by profession', solemnised the secular games by killing in the arena 32 elephants, 10 eland, 10 tigers, 70 lions, 30 leopards, 10 hyenas, 1 rhinoceros, 1 hippopotamus, 10 giraffes, 20 zebras, and 10 wild horses. We also read that the Emperor Probus in one day in A.D. 281 sacrificed 1,000 ostriches, 1,000 stags, 1,000 fallow-deer, and 1,000 wild boar; while on the following day 100 lions, 100 lionesses, 200 leopards, and 300 bears were massacred in the arena.

While some of these animals were brought from as far away as India for the games (the younger Gordian paid for ten Indian tigers in addition to thirty African hyenas for his triumph), most of the pachyderms and exotic beasts were brought up from Equatorial Africa along the caravan routes controlled by the Garamantes. Only the traveller who has crossed these empty and often waterless deserts can imagine the enormous difficulties of transporting animals like giraffes and hippopotamuses across the Sahara. They must have been brought in enormous cages carried on carts drawn by oxen; then shipped across the Mediterranean from ports like Leptis Magna.

In short, so valuable was the trans-Saharan caravan trade that the Roman army must have continually sent reconnaissance forces down into the desert, while encouraging the Garamantes, by loaning them engineers from the Third Augusta Legion, to build forts and blockhouses along the caravan routes in order to control the movement of people and trade.

But until European travellers reached the Fezzan in the first decades of the nineteenth century the Empire of the Garamantes remained a semi-mythical country, like the Atlantis of Plato. And even the early explorers who travelled through these ancient lands and saw the monuments along the great Garamantian highways seldom recognised the historical significance of what they saw. This was understandable. The first travellers were soldiers, sailors, and medical men, not professional historians, and they had more important assignments than to prove the existence of a nation which was once thought to exist only on paper. All the same, they caught glimpses of a 'lost world' in their journeys, and the evidence began to mount up that an unknown civilisation lay buried beneath the sand. There were also strange and mysterious monuments still standing, for the explorers report 'ancient and very lofty edifices', inscriptions, rock tombs, rock paintings and engravings, underground water tunnels, pyramids, fortresses, and even abandoned cities. Dr. Heinrich Barth, marching along the northern fringes of the Mourzouk Sand Sea in the year 1850, summed up the mystery of the country in this report:

> We obtained a distant glance towards west south west of the ruins of a fortress called Ksar Sharaba, the history of which, as it is connected with the struggles of yore between the Tebu and the inhabitants of Fezzan, would be full of interest if it could be made out distinctly.

It is over a hundred years since Barth wrote his report, yet we still know nothing about the fortress city of Sharaba which lies out there in the desert gradually sinking beneath the sand. In the first place, perhaps not more than a few score European travellers have visited the site in any case, as it lies off the caravan routes in one of the more inaccessible pockets of the Mourzouk Sand Sea. I found that it could be reached by Land Rover, with the help of a Tuareg guide who knew which valleys through the dunes were passable. On arriving, I could do nothing but photograph the mysterious ruins into which no archaeologist has yet sunk a spade. Yet perhaps here, at this lost city, lies hidden evidence of the rise and fall of the Garamantian Empire.

In point of fact, archaeological research in the country of the Fezzan has only just begun and could not be undertaken at all as long as the Sahara remained forbidden territory to Europeans. Throughout the nineteenth century, Tuareg banditry and religious fanaticism made travel for Christians particularly hazardous, even when they were disguised as Moslems. Such early explorers had to use the greatest caution in making measurements or observations, and even in writing up their notes and diaries, for their fellow travellers' suspicions were easily aroused. Hence Frederick Hornemann, one of the first to cross the desert, was in serious trouble for showing too much interest in the ruins of the great temple of Jupiter Ammon at Siwah; and René Caillié had to draw his plans of the mosques at Timbuktu under his robe.

In short, scientific exploration of the desert, and particularly of the Fezzan, was not really possible until the Italian occupation of Libya in 1913. Then, like the French in adjacent Algeria and the British in Egypt, the Italians set up a Department of Antiquities in the Colonial Administration and began a methodical survey of their territory, periodically publishing their findings in special monographs. Without these departments staffed by dedicated scholars who combined physical courage with erudition, we would still know very little of the history of the Sahara and next to nothing of the Garamantes. Fortunately, a team of top-flight Italian scholars was sent to the Fezzan in 1933 expressly to try to solve the mystery of this vanished nation; and while the expedition spent only three and a half months in the field, it was excellently led and organised. The archaeologists were relieved by the army of all the problems of transport, supplies, and security and were able to survey the whole length of the Wadi el Ajal from Ghat to Sebha—in other words, the main east–west highway of the

Central Sahara. The results of this expedition were eventually published by the Accademia Nazionale dei Lincei of Rome in a handsomely illustrated monograph called *Scavi Sahariani*.[1]

Saharan Excavations is still the repository of almost all our archaeological knowledge of the Garamantes and, up to the present when a small British expedition has taken up the work where the Italians left off over thirty years ago, our only source of evidence. But the evidence, once the archaeologist's spade turned over the sand, was found to be considerable: some 100,000 small circular rock graves at the base of the escarpments; two long lines of royal tombs; two cemeteries of pyramid tombs; a Roman mausoleum; Roman villas; the vestiges of ancient Garama, capital of the Garamantes; the irrigation system of water tunnels; forts and towers located deep in the desert; and hundreds of artifacts ranging from coins to stone offering tables. From this evidence it is now possible to determine at least the outlines of the lost civilisation.

1. *Monumenti Antichi*, Vol. XLI, 1951.

The desert Tuareg still wear the veil—symbol of their now vanishing way of life

A deserted lake, for it contains none of the 'worms' which form, with dates, the staple diet of the Dawada

The lake at Mandara can only be entered by women, who fish for the 'worms' with seines

The ‘worms’ are baked into lumps in the sun and eaten dry or in a mush

A Dawada father and his daughter. All Dawada females wear black. The women cover their faces

Typical Dawada children outside their *zeriba*, a hut made of palm fronds set in the sand

Left to right: The headman of Mandara, the author, and Abdul Rassig, his guide into the Country of the Worm-Eaters

Above: Rock paintings of the Acacus, depicting various periods, including hunters, horned cattle, and the four-horse chariot of the Garamantes

Opposite: The Acacus Mountains, once the home of prehistoric hunters and herders, now inhabited by a few Tuareg nomads

Tuareg camel caravans are an increasingly rare sight, even in remote parts of the Sahara

8 *The Empire of the Garamantes*

The Garamantes appear to have invaded North Africa some time in the third millennium B.C., bringing with them their chariots, horses, metal weapons, and certain religious customs from their original homeland somewhere in Asia Minor. They were, by Greek or Roman standards, barbarians, but not savages. They were ruled by chieftains and priests, and their economy was based on war and slavery, as was the economy of barbarians all over the known world. War meant flying raids on weaker nations—the pattern of history from time immemorial. In the case of the Garamantes, once they were established along the Libyan littoral, these raids eventually took the form of a full-scale invasion of the Negro nations to the south. The rewards of victory were fertile territory and an enslaved people to work it: that is, a labour force to maintain the water tunnels, cultivate the gardens, and build fortresses and defence towers along the caravan routes which the conquerors now exploited for purposes of trade.

Compared with the pastoral people they had invaded, the Garamantes were advanced, though their religion, art, and technical skills were, for the most part, foreign importations, acquired in their contact with civilised nations like the Greeks, the Egyptians, and, later, the Romans. By the first century B.C. they were barbarians in name only and far more evolved than, say, the barbarians of northern Europe. But what is puzzling is that so far no evidence of their language, either spoken or written, has been found. Not a single inscription has come to light. Yet from earliest times, they had close contacts with the Egyptians to the east and the Carthaginians to the north-west; and finally a long alliance with the Romans.

All three of these people had a written language, and it seems inconceivable that the Garamantes were ignorant of some kind of script.

In the total absence of inscriptions, let alone a literature, almost all we know of them comes from their tombs whose furniture tells us something of what they possessed in this world, and what they expected in the next. In the simplest tombs, which consist of a round pile of rocks over a burial chamber, we find a few characteristic trinkets: that is, coarse pottery, beads made from little bits of rock that glitter, and ornaments of painted ostrich egg shells. In the tombs of the Garamantian kings, on the other hand, the Italian archaeologists found Roman dishes, Alexandrian glass, and goblets of native manufacture—the remains of burial chambers which had undoubtedly been looted in ancient times. Outside these tombs stood altars in the form of horns or obelisks, the former a religious symbol evidently borrowed from the Egyptians and their sun-god Horus; the latter from the Carthaginians and their cult of Tanit. The characteristic offering tables in which were placed the food and drink required by the dead man on his journey to the next world have also been found in great numbers.

So much the artifacts found in the tombs tell us of the religion of the Garamantes before the coming of the Romans. Believing in an after life, they were interred with the treasures they valued in this world, together with such useful household utensils as dishes, cups, wine and oil jars, and lamps. Women were buried with a few of their choice ornaments. Their heaven, therefore, must have been an extension of their earthly life, and their gods the corporeal representations of the spirits they worshipped. These spirits must have been of a sort common to all primitive people whose lives are dominated by powerful physical forces over which they had no control. All travellers in Africa remark on the same profound influence of natural phenomena on the African mind, whether he is Christian, Moslem, or pagan. Sun, winds, clouds, mountains, cliffs, lakes, and wells are still the dwelling place of spirits of djinn who are probably far more influential in popular thinking than the orthodox gods. Just as to-day this deep-seated animism makes the task of European missionaries especially difficult in pagan Africa, so the conversion of the Garamantes to Christianity must have been slow and superficial. And despite the efforts of the powerful prelates of the African Church, this Saharan nation could not have become Christianised in any numbers, for not one of the tombs so far excavated has yielded a single Christian sign or symbol. We may assume, therefore, that the old religion, whatever it was, obtained throughout the Roman period until the Garamantes were obliged, for political reasons, to adopt, along with other confederate nations, the official religion of the Empire.

But accept Christianity they did, for the last we hear of them from classical sources is the statement that they had become converts together with many of the other nations who lived on the fringes of the imperial frontier. Missionaries had undoubtedly followed the merchants as far down as the oases, probably first visiting the capitals of the tribal kings, in the manner of the evangelists who were proselytising northern Europe. Thus, Augustine, the apostle of the English, presented himself to King Aethelberht in person in the year 595. The English king decided to treat him as the ambassador of a great power and, judging from the report of the interview, accorded the Roman priest diplomatic status. Some such reception must have awaited the missionaries sent to the courts and capitals of the African nations, for a Byzantine historian records under the year 569 that the king of the Garamantes concluded a peace treaty with the Empire and that his subjects were 'converted to Christianity'. This event must have been followed by the building of churches in the larger Garamantian towns, just as basilicas had been built all over Roman Africa, even in the oasis of Augila, once a shrine of the powerful cult of Ammon, the chief god of the Egyptian pantheon. So far, however, excavations have not yielded any traces of a Christian temple anywhere within the boundaries of the Garamantian territory.

The absence of material evidence of the Christianisation of this desert nation is not, however, surprising when we remember the paucity of similar finds in Britain, despite the painstaking work of hundreds of British archaeologists, professional and amateur. Professor R. G. Collingwood states that relics of Christianity in Roman Britain are very rare, consisting, in fact, of not much more than the possible foundations of a church at Silchester in Hampshire; fragments of painted plaster purporting to be a Christian mural found at Lullingstone in Kent; some alleged Christian epitaphs; and a few examples of the Chi-Rho monogram, lamps, rings, and other small objects stamped with sacred emblems or formulas.

In view of the scarcity of Christian relics, the probability is that the Gospel, both among the Britains and the Garamantes, was known only to a minority of the population, and that minority mostly Romanised natives who followed the official 'party line'. The slaves, serfs, and peasants far from the urban centres were no doubt indifferent to any and all religions and may never have heard of Jesus Christ. The Christian Fathers have little to say about these barbarians, and almost the only descriptions we have of the ancient African tribes are largely based on hearsay and rumours collected by the Roman historians. These highly sophisticated observers always had the greatest disdain for their fellow men beyond the frontiers and made no pretence at concealing their opinion. Speaking of the various nations of the interior, one writer asserts that they do not have the decency to cover their nakedness; another that they were not only polygamous, but mated indiscriminately like dogs; a third that it was customary for every bride to prostitute herself to all comers on her wedding night; and still a fourth recounting stories of their marching out to make war on the south wind.

One suspects that these reports are based on rumour rather than on facts, all the more so as very few classical historians visited Africa to study the natives at first hand. Those Romans who had actually come into contact with the Garamantes, however, might have given a different picture of the Saharan tribesmen. There must have been a number of merchants who had made the journey down to the capital, Garama, on the export-import business which was sizable enough to warrant special agencies in the African ports at one end and the Italian port of Ostia at the other. The citizens of the coastal cities of Leptis Magna, Oca, and Sabratha had also seen the arrival of the Saharan caravans and they would have undoubtedly admitted that the men from the desert, far from being naked savages, were a strikingly handsome people, tall in stature, elegant in bearing, and formidable as fighting-men. In fact, the Garamantes occasionally attacked or raided the rich ports, requiring the intervention of the regular army to drive them back; and it was as a result of one of these wars that we may have our only idea of what they looked like—if we accept the theory that two of them are depicted on a mosaic in the rôle of prisoners-of-war being thrown to the wild beasts in the arena of Leptis Magna.

In the summer of 1914 Italian archaeologists excavating a large Roman villa at a Libyan village called Zliten, sixty miles east of Leptis Magna, unearthed a series of mosaic pavements which have few equals for beauty or historical interest. In fact, if we had no written records at all, it would be possible to reconstruct large areas of the economic and social life of the African Romans from these Zliten mosaics.

Unfortunately, most of these were destroyed in the 1914–18 war by an Italian naval bombardment; and when the archaeologists returned to Libya eleven years later in 1925 they found 'most of the walls at the finest part of the villa, knocked down; the great mosaic of 24 geometric designs each two feet square, destroyed; other geometric mosaics, gone; the remaining mosaics, all badly damaged; and the work of restoration, completely lost'.[1]

The Italians, however, had photographed their finds in 1914; and it is from these photographs that we can still enjoy such vignettes of a country house, detailed enough for an architect to design and build even down to the landscape gardening; or the picture of an orchestra so meticulously represented that we know what coiffeur the lady organist wore, as we know that her organ was an hydraulic one with twelve pipes, accompanied by two French horns, and that one

1. Salvatore Aurigemma, *I Mosaici di Zliten*, pp. 5–6.

horn player is bearded, the other clean-shaven. And as regards the gladiatorial combats in the arena, the mosaics depict every detail of the fighters' costume down to the folds of their tunics.

Included in these scenes, according to the Italian archaeologist Salvatore Aurigemma, are depictions of Garamantes being thrown to the wild beasts in the arena—the *damnatio ad ferias.*

A word concerning this characteristic Roman punishment. First, the procedure was not always a simple business of letting loose a lion, or tiger, or bear on the defenceless victim in order to despatch him as quickly as possible. To the contrary, there were many refinements to the 'production' which was the special responsibility of a stage-director whose object was to amuse the audience by prolonging the condemned man's agony. Thus, a good-looking prisoner might be given the rôle of Orpheus in the play simply in order to be killed and eaten by a bear as the climax of the drama. The young Christian girl Perpetua was put into the arena at Carthage with her servant to be chased round the ring by a maddened cow as a change from being tossed by the usual wild bull. In Apuleius's novel *The Golden Ass* we read of a woman criminal who was to be sexually ravaged by a donkey before she was killed. And in the Zliten mosaics two victims of the *damnatio* are shown being wheeled into the arena in a curious vehicle rather like a cross between a miniature chariot and a wheelbarrow. They are both standing erect on the platform, tied by their hands and feet to a vertical pole which is fixed into the vehicle. The cart has a long handle or shaft at the rear, so that the *bestiarius*, or animal-keeper, can push it about. The idea, then, was to bind the prisoner to the pole and wheel him into the ring where a leopard especially starved and enraged for the occasion waits for his long-delayed meal. By means of the long handle attached to the back of the cart the *bestiarius* is able to stay in the rear, at the same time turning the cart so that the victim is face to face with the animal which is to tear him to pieces. And to make sure that the leopard doesn't slink away and that the audience isn't disappointed, the *bestiarius* has an assistant who carries a whip in his left hand and a small rattle in his right with which he excites the wild animal to attack.

And this is what we see in the mosaic. The chief animal-keeper is handling two carts with a prisoner standing erect, tied to the pole, in each. The keeper pushes first one, then the other on to the two leopards which have been let loose in the ring. The assistant, with his whip and rattle, has managed to incite one of the beasts to spring on to the chest of one prisoner while he turns the other cart containing the other victim towards the second leopard which is in the act of springing. The first man seems to be already dying from his lacerations; the second man is waiting to die.

The physical appearance of these two men is striking. Too tall to be Italians or Libyans, they have reddish-golden complexions, long, straight hair, aquiline noses, and short, pointed beards. They exhibit, then, all the traits we expect to find in the Garamantes on the basis of what other evidence is available, notably that of the tombs. Such, at any rate, is the conclusion of the Italian anthropologist Sergio Sergi, who measured the skulls found in the Garamantian graves during the Italian 1933 expedition and compared them with the crania of the contemporary Tuareg. His theory is that both peoples belong to the identical racial stock.

9 *After the Arab Conquest*

By the middle of the seventh century A.D. the Arab conquest of North Africa was already foreshadowed in the raids of desert commandos who swept out of Egypt and terrorised the countryside right up to the walls of the Tripolitanian cities. The threat of a massive invasion by the armies of the Prophet must soon have become obvious, yet there seems to have been no concerted or effective preparations for defence on the part of Roman Africa. Such pusillanimity in the face of the destruction of their cities, homes, and their way of life itself can only be explained on the basis of the internal divisions caused by three centuries of warfare between the Christian sects themselves—the orthodox Catholics on one side, the heretical Donatists on the other. In other words, Christianity, far from uniting peoples of North Africa, had divided them. Hence, when the Arabs came out of the east, there were neither Roman legious nor Christian crusaders to stop them. Instead, each city did its feeble best to save itself. The principal resistance to the invaders was eventually organised and led by a Berber queen called Kahina who was said to have been a convert to Judaism—meaning, perhaps, that she was a crypto-Christian. But once she was overwhelmed and her Berber guerilla forces annihilated, the Roman rule and Christian religion alike were doomed in Africa, so that by A.D. 700 the Arab chroniclers were able to report that 'there is no longer found in Ifriqiya either Greeks or Berbers disposed to resist'. The 'Greeks' included the Byzantines, the Italians, and the Romanised Africans; the Berbers, all those mountain and desert tribes who occupied North Africa down to the Sahara Desert.

The last Byzantine outpost on the African continent, Ceuta across the Straits from Spain, fell in A.D. 709 when Count Julian betrayed the fortress to the Arabs.

In company with the cities of the coast, the Garamantes, for their part, appear to have put up no resistance to the invaders, for the Fezzan was easily reduced by the Arab general Okba ibn-Nafi at the head of 400 horsemen, with a supply train of 400 camels carrying 800 goatskins of water.[1] In view of the traditional ferocity of the Saharan nation as warriors and bandits, their collapse in the face of such a small force is one of the puzzles of history. It can perhaps be best explained by the chaos in civil and military affairs which characterised the end of the Roman Empire all over the Western world. There were no longer any legions to guard the frontiers, and the big centres of Roman civilisation—the Mediterranean ports and provincial cities of the coastal plains—cowered behind their walls and allowed the Arab invaders to sweep at will through the countryside.

By A.D. 668, Okba ibn-Nafi had his headquarters at Syrte, almost mid-way between Benghazi and Tripoli, and from here he swooped south on flying raids down into the Fezzan, dealing in characteristic fashion with the opposition. It is clear from the laconic reports of the Arab historians that he had no difficulty in subduing the petty kings of the desert tribes and towns as far south as Garama and even beyond.

> Having cut off the ear of the king of Waddan [Ibn-Khaldoun writes] and exacted a tribute of 360 slaves, he [Okba] desired to know what kind of country lay beyond Waddan. They told him of Germa, capital of the whole Fezzan. Leaving Waddan, he arrived after a march of eight nights on the outskirts of Germa whose inhabitants he invited to embrace Islam. They agreed, and he called a halt six miles from the town.
>
> When the king of the Garamantes came out from Germa to meet Okba, the Arab horsemen rode in between the king and his escort, forcing them to dismount and to walk on foot, the six

1. See, Ibn-Khaldoun, *History of the Conquest of Egypt*, Vol. I, Appendix vi. pp. 308 ff.

> miles to where Okba was camped. Since the king was sickly, he arrived in an exhausted state, spitting blood.
>
> 'Why do you treat me like this after I have yielded to you?' the Garamantian king asked.
>
> 'It will teach you a lesson not to make war on the Arabs,' Okba replied as was his custom; and he sent the king back to Egypt in chains.[1]

This sickly monarch, who was apparently incapable of fighting or commanding his troops, was undoubtedly the last king of the Garamantes, for monarchs of this nation are never heard of again after the Arab conquest of the Fezzan, a conquest which took Okba and his 400 cavalry only five months to complete. Only one castle gave him any trouble, 'a great fortress on the top of an escarpment and capital of the country of Kouar'. Okba reached this outpost after marching fifteen nights. Arriving under the walls of this castle, he began the siege, but at the end of a month gave up the attempt; and falling on the other castles, he captured another king and cut off his finger 'to give him a lesson'. He also imposed his usual tribute of 360 slaves and asked his usual question: Were there any inhabitants to the south?

The defenders replied that they had nobody with them to act as guides and no idea of the route. Okba therefore decided to retrace his steps and arriving unexpectedly at the fortress of the Kouar, he profited from the darkness to enter. The people had retired to their underground chambers, thinking there was no more danger. Okba thereupon cut the throats of all the men capable of fighting and, taking the children and the booty hidden in the city, he returned the way he came.

The whereabouts of this 'great fortress on the top of an escarpment' is a mystery which has not yet been unravelled, for the remains of Garamantian fortresses lie scattered all over this region of the Fezzan where Okba was campaigning in A.D. 668. We are not told in which direction the Arab commander marched for fifteen nights after he left Germa, but if we assume that his average rate was twenty miles in a night, he would have been somewhere on an arc 300 miles from the

1. op. cit. p. 196.

Garamantian capital, which proves that the Fezzan in the last days of the Roman Empire contained numerous castles and strongholds in regions of the desert which are now completely arid and abandoned. Nor is there any lack of archaeological evidence of the comparative prosperity of the region at this period, for the traveller can see for himself the ruins of the mud-brick and cement fortresses and watch-towers not only along the old caravan routes but in the sand seas. Since some of these strongholds show signs of Roman handiwork, it is clear that they were built, perhaps with the aid of Roman engineers, during the great days of the Garamantes when this desert nation was a confederate of Rome. In contrast, the fact that the last king of Garama came cravenly out of his fortress (which is now being excavated to reveal that it was a fairly massive building of dressed stone) proves that all this part of the then-known world had been lost to the West, as it remained lost for the next thousand years and more. The fortresses which had been erected during the Roman and, later, Byzantine periods as frontier posts to protect the oases, guard the caravan routes, and serve as bulwarks against the raids of the Negro barbarians to the south of the Great Desert, were independently manned by a handful of desert tribesmen whose ignominious death in the underground chambers symbolised the utter collapse of Roman Africa.

And so, within a space of fifty years, almost eight centuries of European rule in North Africa came to a sudden end. The culture, language, Christian religion, and institutions ended with it. By A.D. 717, when the caliph Omar II withdrew the right of freedom of worship, tens of thousands of Christians had renounced their faith and their churches had fallen into ruins which still lie scattered across the upper third of the continent from the Mediterranean to the Sahara. Even cities the size of Leptis Magna were 'now a desert, as though they had never existed'.

During these cataclysmic years many devout Christians had chosen to escape while there was still a chance. Some managed to cross over to Europe, where they complained that they were uncharitably received; some in the westernmost Roman province of Mauretania sailed 200 miles across the Atlantic to Tenerife in the Canary Islands; and some must have fled into the desert and mountains, to regions beyond the reach of even the Arabs. It is reasonable to suppose that Garamantian Christians were among this group, actually surviving with their own language and customs.

This fascinating and provocative theory is partly based on the assumption that descendants of the Garamantes still live within the confines of the ancient empire in the persons of the Tuareg. We can understand why when it is recalled how travellers from the time of the earliest explorations of the Sahara have been struck by the marked difference between the Tuareg and all other desert peoples. In the first place they are strikingly taller and straighter than the Berbers, Arabs, or hybrids who are descendants of Arab masters and their Negro slaves. Those Tuareg who call themselves 'nobles' are, on an average, six feet tall, and from what one can see of their faces through the slits in their veils, their complexion is copper-coloured, as it is in the portraits of the two supposed Garamantian prisoners-of-war being thrown to the wild beasts in the Zliten mosaic, though one can only speak of complexion in relative terms, since the Tuareg seldom wash and their skin becomes stained with the navy-blue dye of their face-coverings.

In addition to their unique physical characteristics, the Tuareg have retained their own language and alphabet—the former is tentatively identified with Old Libyan; the latter partially derived from the Punic. Nobody, including the Tuareg, knows anything very positive about either the written language called T'ifinagh, or the spoken language called Temajegh. While the spoken language is still extant, the written language is dying out, for the Tuareg have little use for it. In their heyday, when they were 'Lords of the Desert', writing, like poetry and music, was an accomplishment of the women. The women taught the boys to write, and when the boys became warriors and camel-riders they covered the rocks of the desert with T'ifinagh inscriptions, many of them quite long ones. I never found anybody who could read them, though my Tuareg guides would try and, in some cases, were able to make out a word, or thought they could. But it is an exceedingly difficult script, full of abbreviations and devoid of all vowels except the Alif, or *a* sound. It can also be written from left to right, right to left, up to down, down to up, and in spirals. And it is said of it that the reader must know the sense of the writing before he can hope to understand it.

It is a serious loss to our knowledge of Tuareg history that we cannot read the many ancient inscriptions found all over the desert, for it is possible that some of them would give us key facts to this nation's origin and provenance. But the difficulties of deciphering these inscriptions have so far proved insurmountable. For the Tuareg orthography is even more incomplete and defective than either the Arabic or Hebrew script, due to the fact that these people never use books written in their own language and have never employed T'ifinagh for scientific purposes. We ask what is the origin of such a language? Whence did the Tuareg derive it? Where did the letters which are not Punic come from? And is it possible that it represents the speech of the old Garamantes?

Turning to the social structure of the Tuareg, we find that this is based on an ancient tribal system obviously refined by contact with civilised peoples. Thus, the community is divided into nobles, serfs, and slaves, for women as well as for men. To what extent this class system is derived from the Garamantes is, of course, purely hypothetical, since we know little or nothing about the internal organisation of the latter nation. Yet there are some shreds of evidence which seem to substantiate the conjecture. For instance, the sixth-century African poet-historian Corippus describes the weapons of the Garamantes almost precisely as those that the Tuareg warrior, until recently, took with him on a raiding party.[1] These weapons were the sword, spear, shield, and dagger—the combat implements of the Roman legionnaire and, for that matter, *les armes blanches* of the medieval knight. In fact these weapons were so traditional among the Tuareg that they despised modern inventions like the rifle, which, they said,

1. Corippus, *Johannis seu De Bellis Libycis*, IV, 1065–83.

enabled a coward to kill the bravest man. Armed in this characteristic fashion, the Tuareg, for as long as they were 'lords of the desert', indulged in their favourite sport, which was the 'hit-and-run' raid, a type of brigandage strikingly similar to that condemned by St. Augustine. Indeed, Augustine's description of the raiders of his day recalls still another custom of the Tuareg, for he explicitly states that the desert raiders of his time surrounded themselves with women and young girls and passed the nights in drunkenness and debauchery. We seem to have here a scandalised reference to the Tuareg 'courts of love' at which unmarried girls, when they are in a state called *asri*, sleep with as many men as take their fancy, particularly after the warriors return from a campaign or battle.

We know, too, that these brigands of Augustine's day were Christians (though heretics according to the Catholic Church), and if we accept the theory that the fifth-century raiders (called *circumcelliones*, or 'prowlers around farmhouses') were the ancestors of the Tuareg, we may have an explanation of the curious Christian associations still found among the Veiled Men. Certainly the vestiges of Christian ritual and dogma which have apparently survived the conversion of the Tuareg to Mohammedanism are otherwise difficult to account for. How else, for instance, are we to interpret their predilection for the cross which adorns their shields, sword hilts, camel headpieces, saddle pommels, ceremonial spoons, and a variety of metal ornaments?

The use of the cross by the Tuareg is unique among Moslems, to whom the symbol, in any case, is specifically proscribed; and there is no satisfactory explanation of this usage other than that it is a relic of their former Christian heritage. Other vestiges of the old religion are seen in a number of words characteristic of Christian terminology and evidently derived from the Low Latin that was once the *lingua franca* throughout Roman Africa. The most obvious words are *Mesi* for 'God' (thought to be a variant of 'Messiah'); *angelous* for 'angel' (Latin, *angelus*); and about half a dozen other bastardised ecclesiastical terms.

But even more suggestive than the cross and the Christian expressions is the status of women among the Tuareg. For not only are these desert people monogamous, but the wife is treated as the equal of her consort, even to the extent of going unveiled, choosing her own husband, inheriting his position in the tribe, and owning her own property. Such concessions to women are contrary to orthodox Islamic law and verge on the heretical.

It could, of course, be argued that women have obtained a degree of emancipation in other non-Christian societies, but such does not seem to have been the case anywhere else in Africa. Among pagan Africans, as among Moslems, women have few more rights than serfs, and in many places are treated no better. The Tuareg, to the contrary, seem to have gone to the opposite extreme and to have idealised women somewhat in the manner that medieval knights idealised their ladies. Admired and respected, the well-born Tuareg woman devoted herself to the arts of music and poetry, and the concerts she gave in her tent were attended by warriors from all over the desert. Once married, she proved faithful, though if she were otherwise her husband had the duty of avenging his honour in blood. Where, we may ask, did the Tuareg derive this respect for women unless from some tradition inherited from a former Christian belief? Certainly not from the religious or social precepts of their neighbours, African pagans on the one hand, Arab Moslems on the other.

It is, then, these peculiarities of culture that make the Tuareg distinct from all other North African peoples—Berbers, Arabs, Negroes, and those of mixed blood—and strengthen the conjecture that they are actually a remnant of that lost nation, the Garamantes. Customs, language, and their very attitude to life make them a separate entity, though it should be quickly pointed out that we are now speaking of them in an almost historical sense. For each decade, or, for that matter, each year, disrupts their social and economic life: it is obvious now that their old culture is about to be submerged under the tide of events. Yet the threat does not arise from a deliberate attempt to change them, or from any overt pressure by the new African governments in whose territories they survive. Most Tuareg are, in any case, too far from the urban centres to be affected by policies of education, industrialisation, modernisation, and so forth. They keep pretty much to their old camel-grazing grounds in the desert and mountains, and will be found in regions which town-dwellers would regard as an uninhabitable wilderness.

But two irresistible forces militate against their survival as 'knights of the desert' in the second half of the twentieth century: one is the conquest of the sands by mechanised transport and the resultant collapse of the camelline economy on which the whole Tuareg way of life is based; the other is the discovery of oil all over the desert and the wealth it brings to all those connected with its exploitation.

The effect of these developments is that the Tuareg has lost his *raison d'être*. There is no longer any place for either 'knights' or robber-barons in a desert constantly crossed by cars, trucks, and convoys fitted out with radios, water tanks, canned foods, and most of the amenities of city life. Attacks by bands of warriors mounted on camels and armed with long lances and great shields of hide would merely seem absurd in the sand seas today. They were once, however, the motivating force in a Tuareg nobleman's life. So, too, his herds of camels, which were his principal way of estimating wealth, are superfluous, no longer needed to convey merchandise across the desert from Negroland to the Mediterranean. The slave caravans, too, have long since ceased, together with the enormous salt caravans of the last century. The Tuareg and his camel are no longer needed.

What is happening is the adaptation by some of the tribes to the modern world in so far as it has reached the oases, so that the traveller finds many Tuareg today, including those of noble birth, settled in the villages, living in *zeribas*, or wattle huts, and seldom travelling as far as the next oasis. Some, as headmen of their community, are able to keep up an appearance of their old aristocratic way of life; others gradually settle down to the routine procedures of the market-gardener. They remain conscious of their racial origin, but, no longer nomadic, allow themselves to be assimilated into the community life. Some have already discarded the veil, and once a Tuareg has done this, he may almost be said to have renounced his tradition. He is seldom now seen mounted on a white camel, carrying his lance and shield, riding over the sands and looking out through the slits in his face-cloth.

The last Tuareg who cling to their old culture and absent themselves from contact with civilisation do not, unfortunately for our romantic notions, strike the observer as 'noble savages'. They are manifestly so harassed by poverty, malnutrition, and disease that their obstinacy in living in such wildernesses as the Tassili-n-Ajjer and the Acacus, far from seeming romantic, appears almost irrational—at least, until one remembers that, like the Dawada, they cannot escape their surroundings in any case. Yet the old-fashioned Tuareg has no apparent desire to do so, for he is still convinced that the grim struggle to survive is worth it. What does it matter if he is hungry and cold if he is free—not confined to a hovel made of mud bricks and to the few sandy lanes of an oasis—or shut in like Europeans in their cities; but free to ride his camel to the other side of the mountain or even across an immense sand sea, if he feels like it? And as he oscillates back and forth in his saddle, he glories in this freedom and honestly considers the life of other men not worth living. He is a free man; they are prisoners of their surroundings.

Thus it is that progress drives the more obstinate Tuareg deeper into the wastelands of the Sahara Desert and makes his non-conformist way of life even more archaic. It is incontrovertible that he cannot survive much longer as a picturesque camel-rider, occupied with warrior pursuits and 'courts of love' and depending for his more humdrum needs on serfs and slaves. He is doomed to become a market-gardener, ditch-digger, or truck-driver for the oil companies. I have never yet seen a Tuareg in the neat but ill-made Western suits that the city-dwelling Libyans, for instance, wear as a symbol of their modernity. The veiled men cling obstinately to their long black or white robes, even when they are members of a labour gang, with pick-axe in hand. But, even so, the old image of them is becoming vaguer and, as one would expect, is already being dressed up for tourists to the more accessible oases, in the manner of folk dancers who, once a year in the holiday season, put on a spectacle to remind us of a past that has actually disappeared along with the stage coach.

In this sense the Tuareg may be said to belong to a lost world, along with their probable ancestors, the Garamantes.

BOOK FOUR

Christianity in Africa

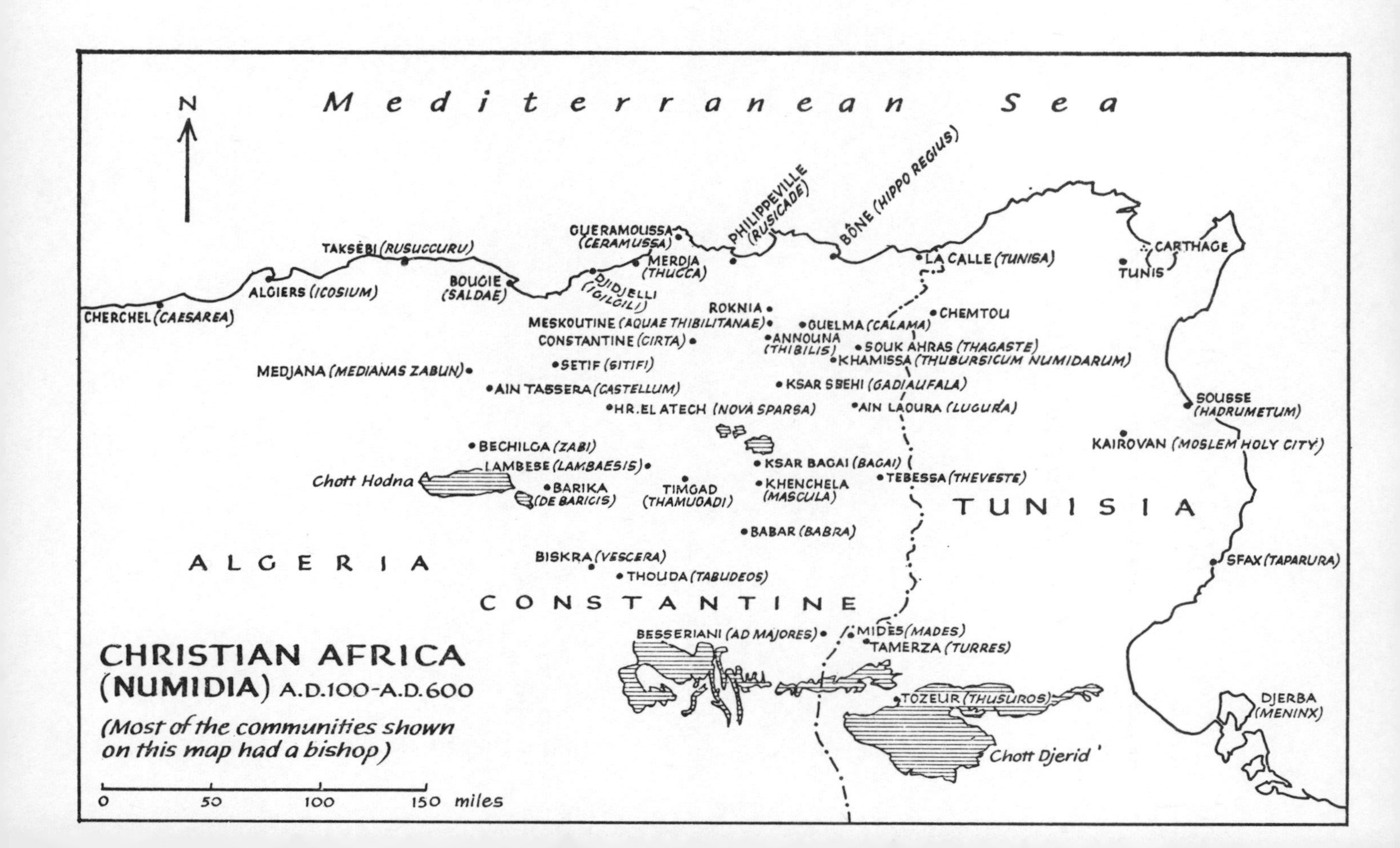
N
Mediterranean Sea
CHERCHEL (CAESAREA)
ALGIERS (ICOSIUM)
TAKSÈBI (RUSUCCURU)
BOUGIE (SALDAE)
DJIDJELLI (IGILGILI)
GUERAMOUSSA (CERAMUSSA)
MERDJA (THUCCA)
PHILIPPEVILLE (RUSICADE)
BÔNE (HIPPO REGIUS)
LA CALLE (TUNISA)
CARTHAGE
TUNIS
ROKNIA
MESKOUTINE (AQUAE THIBILITANAE)
CONSTANTINE (CIRTA)
GUELMA (CALAMA)
ANNOUNA (THIBILIS)
CHEMTOU
SOUK AHRAS (THAGASTE)
KHAMISSA (THUBURSICUM NUMIDARUM)
MEDJANA (MEDIANAS ZABUN)
SETIF (SITIFI)
AIN TASSERA (CASTELLUM)
HR. EL ATECH (NOVA SPARSA)
KSAR SBEHI (GADIAUFALA)
AIN LAOURA (LUGURA)
SOUSSE (HADRUMETUM)
KAIROVAN (MOSLEM HOLY CITY)
BECHILGA (ZABI)
LAMBESE (LAMBAESIS)
Chott Hodna
BARIKA (DE BARICIS)
TIMGAD (THAMUGADI)
KSAR BAGAI (BAGAI)
KHENCHELA (MASCULA)
TEBESSA (THEVESTE)
TUNISIA
BABAR (BABRA)
ALGERIA
BISKRA (VESCERA)
THOUDA (TABUDEOS)
SFAX (TAPARURA)
CONSTANTINE
BESSERIANI (AD MAJORES)
MIDES (MADES)
TAMERZA (TURRES)
TOZEUR (THUSUROS)
Chott Djerid
DJERBA (MENINX)
CHRISTIAN AFRICA
(NUMIDIA) A.D.100-A.D.600
(Most of the communities shown on this map had a bishop)
0
50
100
150 miles

10 *The Coming of the Gospel to Roman Africa*

The Berber village of Hamman Meskoutine, which means in Arabic 'the Accursed Baths', lies about seventy miles to the east of the city of Constantine in northern Algeria. The old guide-books written for more leisurely days, when well-to-do tourists wandered through the French colony with their picnic hampers and sunshades, gives particulars of how to arrive at Hamman in comfort. The traveller took the train at Constantine, being advised to board a special carriage to avoid changing; and after a three-hour journey through *un pays dénudé et sans intérêt* arrived at Hamman Meskoutine, to be met at the station by a barouche which conveyed him up a short incline to the Hotel Thermal.

Today there is only an occasional train to the spa, the barouches have gone, and though the hotel remains, it would scarcely rate even the old guide-book classification of 'modest'. Yet the ghosts of the French colonists still haunt it, despite the broken-down tennis court enclosed within a rusty wire fence behind which is dumped the hotel rubbish. The garden, in which bits and pieces of Roman altars and statuary stand slightly askew, are reminders of still other colonists who no doubt had their hotel, since they, the Romans, certainly used the adjacent baths. Inside the *Thermal* the dining-room and bedrooms are not such as the French *colons* and their wives and children would have eaten or slept in: the dining-room has oilcloth on the tables; the bedrooms have no handles to the doors, no water for the washbasins or bidets, and no linen on the beds. However, I made myself as comfortable as I could in this dilapidated caravanserai and just before midnight decided to visit the bathing establishment. I descended the steps into the steaming *hamman* to wait in the lamplight with the Algerians and their crying babies in a shadowy cavern with clouds of steam rising from pits and gullies in the floor. When my turn came I was shown into a small concrete cubicle in which stands a deep tub fitted with antique taps. The near-boiling water filled the tub, and one sits in it amid the gloom. So sat the Roman legionaries who were always being scrubbed down in spas all over the Roman world, from Bath in Britain to Hamman Meskoutine in Numidia. So sat the warriors of the Arab general Okba ibn-Nafi, who finished off the Roman civilisation. And so sat the French *colons* until their turn, too, came to pass on.

The Baths of the Damned have changed very little from prehistoric times. Here, from deep underground, erupt 25,000 gallons of near-boiling water per minute. Heavily charged with calcium, the steaming flow has formed those curious obelisks which Arab mythology tells us are the petrified bodies of a rich and powerful man and his sister whom he insisted on marrying. At the moment of these incestuous nuptials, says the legend, the elements protested by tearing the face of the earth apart; and when calm was restored there stood the guilty pair turned to stone.

What we see today are many calcite formations in the shape of cones standing in a landscape of livid rocks among which the steaming jets bubble up and flow down slopes which have turned into frozen waterfalls—the celebrated cascades of Hamman Meskoutine. Such a splendid natural spa with its opportunities for therapeutical baths and cures ranging from rheumatism to syphilis has naturally been known and exploited since the Stone Age. Not far away, on the mountains over which the wild boar still roam, neolithic men built their rock tombs at the necropolis of Roknia with its dolmens and funeral vaults. A friendly Algerian farmer who accepts a lift along the deserted road conducts me across fields and along the ledges of cliffs to show me these prehistoric monuments, of which there are said to be 3,000 dolmens and 400 rock tombs. They are not, alas, very interesting, as most of the former seem to have tumbled down and all the latter appear to be empty. In any case, one needs a vivid imagination to be inspired by neolithic burial grounds.

The numerous Roman ruins in the region, on the other hand, are far more evocative, and it is to one of these forgotten cities, a place called Thibilis, that I am next led by two Berber boys who emerge from an adjacent farm; and while they run about me, proffering handfuls of coins, I look for the Christian church which St. Augustine himself may have visited 1,400 years ago. The basilica of Thibilis is also unique in that it is reputed to have a cross engraved on the cornice stone of the entrance. It is rare to find such a symbol in Moslem Africa, despite the ruins of hundreds of Christian churches, for the sign is anathema to Mohammedans, who erase it whenever they can. But the cross on the stone above the entrance to the Thibilis church has somehow escaped, and, upon seeing it, the traveller finds it easier to visualise North Africa as a Christian land. Did St. Augustine, one wonders, actually preach from the ruins of the altar on the occasion of his mission to this hotbed of Donatism? He tells us in a letter that he made the 200-mile journey from Carthage to nearby Thurbursicum Numidarum in order to meet Bishop Fortunius —'a journey that I decided to make on account of his age'— and writes:

> As soon as we sat down for our conference, the noise increased, and a large crowd assembled. But it was obvious that very few of the bystanders were capable of discussing anything in a reasonable manner and fewer still wanted to debate such an important issue with good sense, let alone piety. Still others had turned up just to see our interview, as one goes to the theatre to see a show, not at all in a mood of Christian devotion for the purpose of seeking spiritual guidance. To the contrary, they would neither give us a chance to speak, nor would they themselves speak to me respectfully, or at least with reason and logic. No! Each of them let himself be carried away by the violence of his passions. The uproar was deafening, and neither of us was able to obtain a moment's silence, either by our prayers, or even

threats. The crowd's behaviour became so obstreperous that we were forced to break off our conference and finished by being smuggled out of Thurbursicum to a nearby house.[1]

The saint has given us a vivid description of a Roman-African city in the fifth century, while at the same time epitomising the passion and fury which had divided the African Church for 200 years and which was to go far beyond the shouting and shaking of fists which marked that day in Thurbursicum Numidarum. Perhaps the same scene was repeated in Thibilis; and, if it was, one cannot escape the suspicion that it was the African Christians who brought the disasters of the Vandal and Arab invasions upon themselves by refusing to listen to their own saints.

The church at Thibilis, then, is a melancholy place, all the more so since the excavations made on the site seem to be of the unfinished kind so characteristic of the hundreds of North African Roman cities superficially turned over with the spade and then abandoned. Nor is the mood dispelled back at Hamman Meskoutine which also has its Christian church—this one built by the French—in an almost comparable state of dilapidation, so that it tells us much the same story as the Roman basilica at Thibilis. In fact, the French church is already as neglected as the nearby shrine of a local pre-Roman god called Bacax. But since the building is strongly constructed and stands on a rock, vestiges of the church may be found in a thousand years' time; and for the archaeologists of that period we record that this small basilica was built in 1951 and dedicated to SS. Paul and Stephen. As the nearby tomb with its marble slab, decorated with a cross, is used as a sheep fold, it is doubtful whether it will survive as long.

The Roman temple at Thibilis and the French church at Hamman Meskoutine, then, are reminders that the two attempts made within the last nineteen centuries to establish Christianity in North Africa both ended in failure. Neither armies, administrators, nor missionaries succeeded in their objective of conquering this region of the continent for Christ.

1. St. Augustine, *Epistolae*, XLIV (A.D. 398).

Yet their failure to do so is one of the paradoxes of history, especially when it is realised that Africa was one of the most active and vigorous strongholds of the Christian Church from the middle of the second to the end of the seventh century. During that period it produced more bishops, basilicas, congregations, and martyrs than any other Roman province. The cross was triumphant from the Red Sea to the Atlantic Ocean and, for all we know, Christian evangelists had crossed the Nubian and Sahara Deserts to bring the good tidings to the savages of Central Africa. Yet by A.D. 750 this religion, which had become the creed of the whole civilised Western world, was as moribund throughout Africa as the worship of the old gods of Carthage. It has never, despite the efforts of churches and states, ever been able again to take root in the upper third of the continent.

The beginnings, like the end, are still a matter of conjecture, for we have no record of a St. Paul visiting Africa with the new gospel, or of a Joseph of Arithamea who, we are told, brought Christianity to Britain, having floated across the Channel on the shirt of his son. We can only surmise that it was Jewish merchants who brought the news of the Messiah to the south Mediterranean shores, for these traders were in close contact with their co-nationals in ports like Antioch, Tyre, Alexander, Cyrene, and Carthage. The crucifixion of Jesus was recounted in Jewish communities as another typical example of Roman oppression, the news of which spread quickly through the Israelite quarters in all the big cities and from the Jews to their Gentile neighbours. Many of these were merchants and traders with no love for their Roman overlords whose oppressive taxation was always a cause for discontent.

In the beginning these potential rebels may have sympathised with the gospel of Jesus more as an expression of their political than their religious faith; and so, though they called themselves Christians, they were regarded by the authorities as another sect of the Jews, the most stubborn and nationalistic of the subject peoples. On the other hand, to other large though inarticulate groups in society, Christ's teachings transcended narrow political and nationalistic boundaries and offered, for the first time in history, hope for a better life. One such group included by implication the millions of oppressed men who existed under the surface of Roman society, without rights as citizens or dignity as individuals. The slaves, the serfs, the poor and lowly—all such semi-outcasts derived scant comfort from the pagan gods and philosophies, while the gospel of the Son of Man sounded to them like a clarion call to unite as brothers to overthrow an old order based on tyranny.

The second group to whom the promise of a new dispensation made a powerful appeal consisted of women, whatever their status in society; and, indeed, the records show that well-born women were among the earliest converts to the new religion. We hear of the conversion of Domitilla, niece of the Emperor Domitian; of Priscilla, the wife of the Consul Acilius Glabrio; and Lucina, a member of the Pomponian clan, all becoming Christians during the first century; and many ladies of the imperial household were overt or secret sympathisers even during the worst days of the persecutions.

There were two reasons. First, women had played a memorable part in the life of Jesus, so much so that they were entitled ever afterwards closely to identify themselves with the Christian crusade. And, secondly, even women who knew little about theological controversies were intuitively attracted to a doctrine which was based on mercy and love, as contrasted with the pagan creeds which emphasised, for the most part, masculine attributes like law-giving, wisdom, martial valour, patriotism, and the like; or reduced love to the level of mere physical indulgence; or ignored the virtues of mercy and pity altogether. The life as well as the teachings of Jesus evinced a quality of gentleness which was markedly absent in the behaviour of the classical divinities. Thus, a religion based on mercy, gentleness, and love was bound to be enthusiastically welcomed by women living in the quasi-serfdom of pagan society.

Christianity, therefore, with its revolutionary moral and social philosophy, spread rapidly throughout the Empire, secretly admired or openly professed by all who felt themselves the victims of injustice. Even so, the ruling classes were not at first seriously alarmed by either the precepts or the effects of the new creed; and inasmuch as the majority of Christians were of humble status, or women, the pagan leaders, rulers, philosophers, and intellectuals alike underestimated the highly explosive spiritual force that had appeared in their midst. To them, the Nazarene sect (as they thought of it) was merely another Oriental superstition for which they had the greatest contempt. If it originated in Asia Minor, they argued, it was bound to be either licentious, cruel, ridiculous, or disgusting. And, indeed, serious-minded Romans had reason to despise these sects whose priests were too often either perverts or swindlers, while every Roman, for that matter, could produce examples of the depravity of Oriental cults which the authorities from the earliest Republican days had tried to suppress. In vain. The deities imported from Asia Minor and Egypt were far more popular than the official gods of Rome, so much so that a priest of Ba'al could actually become emperor in the person of a young pervert called Elagabalus. Once this youth had assumed the purple, he actually put into practice the tenets of his Syrian religion and proceeded to subject the imperial city to a display of debauchery such as it had not witnessed even in the reign of Nero. He prostituted himself like a temple catamite; proclaimed himself a woman; 'married' one of his army officers (who was encouraged publicly to abuse his 'wife'); painted his face, affected exotic headgear, and wore jewelled shoes; and appeared in public as a dancer. And even if Elagabalus did not last long (he was murdered in his mother's arms at the age of eighteen) he lived long enough to demonstrate the real nature of a typical Oriental religion.

To the educated Roman, then, all cults originating in

Phoenicia, Egypt, Syria, Persia and Palestine were, by definition, suspect, since those which were not orgiastic were brutal in their ritual. Such were the religions associated with Astarte, Aphrodite, Dionysius, Serapis, Silenus, Pan, Attis, Ba'al, and others, whose ceremonies culminated in excesses which all right-thinking citizens condemned as anti-social. Even worse were those brutal Phoenician gods who demanded the sacrifice of children, so that as late as A.D. 130 the Emperor Hadrian had to forbid these human sacrifices.

It is not surprising, therefore, that the authorities were wary of this latest Semitic religion called Christianity and suspected its adherents of malpractices which were invariably characteristic of other Oriental sects. Certain tenets by the Founder seemed to them blatantly anarchistic—sayings like, 'If any man cometh unto me and hateth not his father and mother, and wife and children and brother, he cannot be my disciple'; and, 'The sons of this world marry and are given in marriage, but they that are accounted worthy to attain unto that world and the resurrection from the dead neither marry nor are given in marriage.' It was this apparent condemnation of normal family ties which led the historian Tacitus to speak of *odium generis humani*, or 'detestation of the human race'.

Such, then, was the first reaction of intelligent pagans to the new religion. The unintelligent, as usual, distorted the facts. Christians were accused of sacrificing infants, attending incestuous feasts, worshipping an ass's head, adoring the privates of priests, and venerating a malefactor and his cross.[1] One much repeated slander, which the early apologists had continuously to deny, accused the Christians of eating the flesh of sacrificed babies and afterwards indulging in incest.[2] This libel was also varied by the addition of the macabre detail that the incest took place after dogs, which had candles tied to them, rushed away when food was thrown them, thus

1. For a curious discussion of these charges, see the *Octavius* of M. Minucius Felix, xxviii–xxxii.

2. This legend was revived during the Middle Ages and ascribed, this time by Christians, to non-Christians. Thus, the first act of the Black Mass entailed the eating of a sacrificial baby's flesh; the third act, incestuous love-making.

extinguishing the light. Reasonable men did not believe this nonsense, but condemned the Christians on other grounds; or, rather, dismissed them as one more Oriental sect steeped in superstitition and composed of 'fullers, bakers, foreign slaves, eunuchs, and illiterates'.

But it was one thing for philosophers and scholars to sneer at the new religion and another to prevent it from spreading throughout the Roman world. For the plain fact was that by the second century A.D., the pagan creeds had ceased to be a vital religious force. There was nothing left for ordinary men —those fullers, bakers, foreign slaves, and the like—to believe in, neither the stern morality of Republican Rome on the one hand, nor the Greco-Roman mythology on the other. What was good and true in paganism had finally become systematised into abstruse philosophical theories which appealed to a few lofty spirits whose influence extended little farther than the academies. But it was too late in the tide of history for metaphysics to stir men's minds or for mythology to satisfy their spiritual needs, so that by A.D. 360 not even a wise and good emperor like Julian the Apostate could force men to reverence the old divinities. Zeus was a dead god; Jesus Christ was a living Saviour.

We can assume, then, that the initial appeal of the Christian Gospel was its emphasis on the brotherhood of man, the dignity of the individual, and the promise of eternal life—all of them positive spiritual values which consigned the gods of the classical world to the realm of mythology. But for some reason, probably due to the understandable fears of the early fathers of the Church, the emphasis on loving-kindness and the forgiveness of enemies shifted to a more negative propaganda in which the wickedness of the pagan world and the necessity of Christian suffering became the principal themes. The enemy, far from being forgiven, was to be annihilated in the great cataclysm known as the Last Judgment, while all true believers were to prepare for this awful day by the rule of rigid self-denial.

Even so, this new propaganda appealed strongly to large groups in the community, partly because of the mood of hysteria the imminent destruction of the world must have created; partly because Christians gave indisputable proof of their willingness to suffer even death to atone for the sins of the world. Africans, in particular, were eager to demonstrate their faith by martyrdom, and eyewitness accounts make this clear over and over again.

> How fair a spectacle for God to see [writes Minucius Felix], when a Christian comes face to face with pain, stands matched with threats and punishments and tortures, confronts with a smile the din of death and the hideous executioner, rises to the full height of his liberty in the face of kings and princes and yields to God alone . . . How many of our number have, without a moan, allowed their whole body to be burned to ashes when it was within their power to win release. Nay, our boys and tender women are so inspired to sufferance of pain that they laugh to scorn crosses and tortures, wild beasts and all the paraphernalia of punishment. . . .[1]

This description of Christian fortitude was written some time towards the end of the second century, showing that the State and the Christians had for a long time been at war with each other, the former using the characteristic weapons of torture and judicial murder; the latter the equally characteristic weapons of passive resistance and Christian submission. Yet the champion of the early martyrs and the spokesman for the persecuted sect was far from being a pacifist. Quintus Septimius Florens Tertullianus, otherwise Tertullian, one of the first and certainly one of the greatest of African Christian writers, was a soldier by birth and a fighter by inclination.

Born at Carthage about A.D. 160, the son of a centurion, Tertullian was reared as a pagan. His conversion appears to have been sudden and dramatic, like that of Saul on the road to Damascus. The African, in fact, had a great deal in common with the Jew, since both men began as enemies and ended as soldiers of Christ. They resembled each other in their characters, too: both were militant and uncompromising Christians who helped to shape the future policies of the Church towards

1. Octavius, op. cit., xxxvii.

the austerity which reached its culmination in total asceticism. Both men, again, were obsessed with the nature and extent of sin and with the corruption of the pagan world. Both appear to have been misogynists and tend to blame women for man's fall from grace.

Paul and Tertullian, moreover, were distinguished by their physical as well as their intellectual courage, and it is this absolute fearlessness which gives such enormous force and vitality to their writings. Paul, of course, has the advantage of having been put into English at a time when our language was in its glory; not all of Tertullian's works have been translated. And as very few read his treatises in the original Latin with either ease or pleasure, he remains an obscure figure, despite his enormous contribution to Christian theology. Yet his writings not only give us a vivid picture of Africa during the second century, but enable us to understand why Christianity took such a hold on the minds of men and why the pagan authorities were so alarmed by this phenomenon.

To these authorities a writer like Tertullian was more the spokesman of a political conspiracy than the apologist of a religious creed, for he attacked the very foundations of Roman society in his uncompromising condemnation of all pagan institutions, whatever their origin and whatever their purpose. Thus, he denounces all forms of public entertainment—chariot races, gladiatorial combats, and theatrical performances of every description. They are all idolatrous, sacrilegious, and the work of the Devil. To be even a spectator at a circus, therefore, is to consort by implication with Satan. In fact, even a horse, the moment it enters the arena, passes into the service of the Evil One. Nor does Tertullian stop here, but goes on to assert that the whole world is filled with demons who inhabit every circus, every theatre, every temple, every street, market, tavern, and even home. All these devils and demons are for ever tempting men along the paths of pleasure; but, he writes:

> You, O Christian, will hate these things; for where there is pleasure, there is eagerness, which gives pleasure its flavour.

> Where there is eagerness, there is rivalry: there are also madness, bile, anger, pain, and all things that follow from them and (like them) are incompatible with moral discipline.[1]

Pleasure, then, is condemned ('For you are too dainty, O Christian, if you long for pleasure in this world as well as the other—a bit of a fool into the bargain, if you think this world can yield you pleasure'), and along with it all pagan art and science—the well springs of intellectual pleasure. Thus, poetry is dismissed by Tertullian as mere childish fantasy. 'I cannot believe poets, even when they are wide awake.' He devotes a complete treatise to denouncing painting, though reserving his greatest scorn for philosphy, which he called 'the parent of heresy', while philosophers—'mockers and corrupters of the truth'—stole their theories from the Old Testament.

Already by Tertullian's time, the charge of heresy ('the sin of unbelief') had become a powerful weapon in the armoury of the Christians against their enemies both without and within the Established Church, and one which, ironically, was turned against the centurion's son himself. For, not content with condemning every aspect and institution of pagan life, Tertullian boldly interpreted the sacred doctrine according to his own lights. Hence, while the Church was prepared to allow his description of the soul (which he claimed to have seen) as of the colour and texture of air, it could not countenance his claim that Mary the Mother of Jesus had other children and was the Second Eve. This was heresy, and, as a result, he has never been accepted as a reliable authority on Christian theology and has never been canonised or sanctified. His long and courageous championship of the Church in its most difficult days tends to be overlooked or forgotten.

As for the effect of Tertullian's ideas on circles outside the Church, we may be sure that the supporters of the old pagan system dismissed his attacks on their art, philosophy, and social institutions as the ravings of a religious bigot. The response of those responsible for the maintenance of the system was not

1. Tertullian, *De Spectaculis*, XV.

so offhand. Rather, the administrators took his onslaughts on them at their face value and decided that his writings were neither more nor less than treasonable. In short, the official attitude towards the Christians now hardened: they were charged with being members of a quasi-secret society and of disseminating the following subversive propaganda:

(1) that as the end of the world with the resultant Judgment Day was rapidly approaching, all pagan civic, social, and business activities were a waste of time and effort;
(2) that a man should forsake his wife, a mother her children, a son his parents, in the name of a Jewish malefactor who had been condemned by a Roman court;
(3) that a true Christian should not serve the state in any capacity, either as a soldier, magistrate, or the holder of public office;
(4) that Christians should boycott all pagan religious festivals and public spectacles in order to show their contempt of the Emperor and his representatives;
(5) that Christians should set up an independent government within the State.

It follows that once the authorities had convinced themselves that the Christians were actually intent on overthrowing the régime by outright defiance, it was inevitable that total war would be declared on their sect.

11 *The Martyrs*

The strategy of the pagans in their crusade to crush the Christian rebels now became much more thorough and efficient than the methods employed by previous administrations. From the reign of Nero, Christians had been mistreated without any semblance of justice, and this fact alone had increased their numbers and strength. What, then, was needed was the appearance of legality. The required formula was enunciated in the Edict of Decius (A.D. 250) by which all citizens, irrespective of their race, nationality, or creed were required to perform a sacrifice to the gods in the presence of duly appointed commissioners. Those who made the sacrifice were to be issued with a 'certificate of loyalty', which was the equivalent of a police clearance; those who refused were automatically categorised as 'subversives', to be punished in the case of bishops and priests with death.

The dilemma now facing the Christian population of the Roman world was either to go through the motions of sacrificing in order to save their lives; or to bribe the officials to give them clearance without ever going through the actual ceremony; or to refuse altogether and take the consequences.

The authorities prepared their trap for the Christians with great astuteness, for they guessed that, on the one hand, the most devout and bravest would be caught and killed; and, on the other, the most timid and lukewarm would choose apostasy. They were right, for the African Church, certainly, never wholly recovered from the Edict of Decius, which produced, in addition to the martyrdom of its leaders and the desertion of tens of thousands of its flock, the dissensions and schisms which eventually contributed to the collapse of the religion altogether.

Preparations for the loyalty ceremony were efficient with a view to checking every citizen against the registers; and for this purpose the Capitol was chosen for the test, as it was both a civic centre in every Roman city and the site of the temple of Jupiter, the official protector of the Emperor. To the Capitol following the proclamation of the Edict came a procession of citizens with their thank-offerings, the rich burghers carried in a litter at the head of their families and retainers, who led along a sheep or a bullock for the sacrifice. On entering the temple, the worshipper covered his head with a corner of his toga in the Roman manner and in a loud voice, as he stood before the altar beneath the statue of Jupiter, pledged allegiance to the State and expressly anathematised the Christian religion. After that, the sacrificial animal had its throat cut and was placed on the fire to be roasted. The congregation partook of the burnt meats, a procedure which was particularly offensive to the Christians in view of the sacrament of the Eucharist. These loyalty ceremonies took place in Carthage during the summer days and nights of A.D. 250. All serious work had stopped in the city and the atmosphere was that of a national holiday. Everybody was on the street. All roads led to the Capitol. Here the priests conducted the worshippers through the ceremony which entailed passing by the desks of the clerks who entered their names in the registers as non-Christians and therefore loyal members of the State. A certificate was issued to this effect. Then, those who wished could sit down at the tables which were placed both inside the temple and outside in the courtyard to dine on the roast meats, which were served with bread and wine. This kind of public feasting was extremely popular in Roman cities and could continue for several days at a time, to the delight of the poor and hungry.

But the festival was a nightmare to devout Christians who knew that the alternative to not sacrificing and to not eating the profane meats was imprisonment, exile, torture, and even death. In consequence, the number of apostates ran into tens of thousands, and the magistrates entrusted with the issuance of the certificates of loyalty had to set aside extra days in order to finish the job of enrolment. St. Cyprian who witnessed the event in the unhappy rôle of the head of the African Church describes the interminable procession of citizens towards the Capitol: they included, he laments, Christians bearing floral wreaths, animals for the sacrifice, and pots of incense.

> The rich were followed by troops of slaves, freedmen, and servants. Mothers were carrying their babies, parents leading their children by the hand, husbands dragged along their wives by force . . . One actually saw a woman carried to the temple where her husband and parents held her hands and forced her to throw incense on the fire altar . . .
>
> Even worse things happened. Many of the clergy themselves joined the apostates. The Bishop Repostus led a party of his people to the temple, so did the Bishops Fortunatus, Jovinus, and Maximus.[1]

Cyprian reports a number of cases where God punished the backsliders on the spot. One apostate on pronouncing the blasphemous formula was struck dumb. A woman was taken with atrocious pains in the bath-tub and bit off her tongue. Others went completely off their heads. A young girl dropped dead. A baby who had been taken to the pagan temple by his nurse afterwards refused to open his mouth for the sacred wine of the Eucharist, and when the deacon forced open his lips vomited out the liquid. No better proof, concluded the saintly bishop, could be adduced to demonstrate God's anger.

To add to the disaster and resultant confusion, there was the vexatious problem of whether the *libellatici* (those who had bought their certificate by bribery) were as culpable as their 'lapsed' brethren (those who had actually attended the pagan sacrifice). St. Cyprian thought they were not, for he was anxious to retain them within the fold, particularly as they included many rich and influential families. But the Christians who had not been able to afford to buy their salvation objected

1. St. Cyprian, *Epistulae* and *De Lapsis*.

to this favouritism and the resultant controvery was to split the ranks of the faithful, for Cyprian's leniency towards the *libellatici* suggested that the wealthy were dearer to the Church than the poor. In fact, the controversy of 'lapsed' versus *libellatici* constitutes a turning point in ecclesiastical history.

There were other complications. Those resolute Christians who had refused to sign the loyalty oath and had actually been put into prison were now regarded as both the heroes and rightful leaders of the Christian community to the annoyance of the bishops and deacons who had managed to avoid imprisonment. St. Cyprian, as Bishop of Carthage, warns, therefore, against excessive 'coddling' of the brethren in prison. 'Make your visits to them with modesty and decency', he writes. He was, perhaps, thinking of the counter-propaganda of the pagans who claimed that the prisoners were not only handsomely fed by their women visitors but comforted by them all night long. And as if these innuendoes were not bad enough, certain of the stricter Christian sects maintained that 'coddling' was undesirable for another reason, which Tertullian, with his usual forthrightness, states as follows:

> See how the martyr will come out of prison the same as he went in! In this way [i.e. being fed and comforted by his fellow Christians], he will not know how to kill his flesh or how to suffer the necessary torments. Instead, if his skin becomes as hard as a breastplate, the iron nails will glide over it as over a piece of horn. He won't want to shed his blood at all if you turn his prison into a night club.
>
> Take your Pristinus. Fed like a fighting cock during his detention, he spends all his time at the baths, enjoying all the entertainments offered there, and thinking more about a rub-down than life eternal. When this man comes before his maker, he will be so drunk, he won't feel the iron nails and the only confession he'll be able to make under the divine torture will be a burp.

All of these jibes were most unfair to the many Christians who did attain the crown of martyrdom, despite Tertullian's imputation that their term in jail was one long carousal. On the contrary, the evidence shows that they were subjected to the same tortures that are employed today, notably the sudden arrival in their homes of the secret police, imprisonment with a delayed trial, and the use of 'persuasion' to force them to change their beliefs. The North African Roman cities, both those which have survived across the centuries and those which are now in ruins, nearly all witnessed these travesties of justice.

Constantine in Algeria is such a place, though the tourist who arrives across the mountains by the rather ancient aeroplane and books in at the Europeanised hotels may have difficulty in realising it. For Constantine appears at first view to be a typical Franco-Algerian city: that is, a dual city, one half colonial French (the modern town); the other, Arab-Berber (the Kasbah). It is built on a pinnacle 1,000 feet high and almost encircled by a deep ravine through which flows the River Rummel. A natural fortress, then, since the age of the Numidian kings, and successively occupied by the Romans, the Arabs, the Turks, and the French.

Constantine today has little interest in its ancient history; few of its inhabitants know that their city was once a stronghold of the Christian Church, famed for its martyrs, bishops, and, later, Donatist heretics. The present citizens look forward to a National Socialist Islamic future as promised by their politicians, and this explains the almost continuous processions of banner-waving youths through the streets and squares of the modern city. The boys in their green berets and very short shorts march singing or shouting, and their leaders, sharp-faced men with two days' growth of beard, harangue them from cars fitted with loudspeakers.

Well away from the boulevards and the parades stands the neglected museum left behind by French scholars and administrators. As is usual in towns like Constantine, it is difficult to find out where the museum is or when it is open. But when the traveller enters, he finds himself at once in the presence of the first martyrs, their altars, sacramental tables, and inscriptions. The relics are, for the most part, poor little stones and tablets inscribed with the curious spelling of native Africans who never quite mastered the Latin tongue. A few are splendid mosaics which were set into the walls of a church to record the life and death of some rich member of the congregation. One mosaic is inscribed: 'Asella, a most excellent woman. Rest in Peace.' The formula here is the standard one. Another prefers the beautiful and moving quotation from the pagan poet Virgil:

SALVE ETERNU MIHI MAXIME
FRATER ETERNUMQ VALE
('Salute eternity for me, Brother Maximus, and farewell for ever.')

The most evocative record that the first Christians of Constantine left behind has been seen by very few people and, as the years go by, will probably be seen by fewer until it is lost altogether. This record is an inscription engraved on a rock at the bottom of the deep ravine through which the Rummel flows. It is not an easy spot to reach, and unless the traveller is a rock-climber, he will not venture to reach it from above, for the sides of the ravine go straight down for 1,000 feet—a fall which was extensively used by the beys of Constantine for the despatch of criminals, unfaithful wives, and concubines who displeased them. The place can, however, be approached by a path cut along the precipitous side of the chasm, though this path, once maintained as a tourist attraction, seems to have been abandoned. It leads to the incription celebrating the Passion of the Martyrs of Constantine—an inscription cut into the rock perhaps during the fourth century and reading as follows:

✠ IIII NON SEPT PASSIONE MARTYR
ORVM HORTENSIVM MARIANI ET
IACOBI ΔATI IAPIN RUSTICI CRISPI
TAT ✠ METTUNI BICTORIS SILBANI EGIP
TII SCI DI MEMORAMINI IN CONSPECTU DNI
QVORUM NOMINA SCIT IS QUI FECIT INDXV

which translated seems to read:

> The first of September. In commemoration
> of the Passion of the Martyrs of Hortense (?):
> Marianus and Jacob, Datus, Japin,
> Rusticus, Crispus, Tatus, Mcttun,
> Victor, Silvanus, Egiptius. Now that
> you are in the presence of the Lord,
> remember the names of those who are already
> known to their Creator.

The last sentence is an invocation to the eleven martyrs to bring those who erected the commemoratory plaque to the attention of God, since these names are not mentioned in the dedication out of humility. The martyrs themselves were put to death in A.D. 259 during the persecutions of Valerian. They were arrested by the military police at a farm outside Constantine and brought before the magistrates, charged with being Christians, a 'crime' to which they pleaded 'guilty'. The case against them was then prepared at Constantine with the aid of torture, a usual procedure in Roman jurisprudence, after which they were sent to Lambaesis, headquarters of the Third Augusta legion, for their trial. Here they were condemned to death and executed, together with numerous other Christians, in a ravine near the army camp. Another account, based on the description of the place where Marianus and the others were killed, points to the Gorge of the Rummel as the site of their martyrdom, in which case this dedicatory stone may mark the actual spot where these eleven men died.

We can imagine what it was like to have been a Christian in A.D. 303 in the city of Constantine in Algeria from an actual contemporary report made on May 3rd during the examination of a group of Christians by the chief magistrate of the city, Munatius Felix, described as a 'perpetual flamen' (i.e. a pagan priest) and 'curator' (a municipal officer). It was this official, in his conical white hat made out of the hide of a sacrificed animal, who appeared one day at the meeting house of the Christians of Constantine demanding in the name of the Emperor Diocletian that Bishop Paul and his fellow Christians surrender all their religious books and the articles used in their services, as well as their house. The following account is translated literally from the minutes of Munatius Felix.[1]

When they came to the house in which the Christians were accustomed to assemble, Felix, the perpetual flamen and curator, said to Bishop Paul, 'Bring out the Scriptures and anything else you may have here, as has been commanded, that you may obey the edict.'

Bishop Paul said, 'The Readers have the Scriptures. But we surrender what we have here.'

Felix, the perpetual flamen and curator, said to Bishop Paul, 'Produce the Readers, or send for them.'

Bishop Paul said, 'You know who they are.'

Felix, the perpetual flamen and curator, said, 'No, we don't know them.'

Bishop Paul said, 'The municipal officers know them—Edusius and Junius the Notaries, for instance.'

Felix, the perpetual flamen and curator, said, 'Then we will leave the matter of the Readers, since they will be pointed out by the public officers. As for you, surrender what you have.'

And so, in the presence of Bishop Paul, who remained seated, and of Montanus, Victor, Deusatelius and Memorius, priests; of Mars and Helius, the deacons; with Marcuclius, Catullinus, Silvanus and Carosus the subdeacons standing by with Januarius, Meraclus, Fructuosus, Migginis, Saturninus, Victor, and the rest of the grave-diggers, Victor of Aufidus (the police inspector) made this brief inventory against them:

Two golden chalices, also six silver chalices, six silver goblets, a silver chafing vessel, seven silver lamps, two candelabras, seven short brass candlesticks with their lamps, also eleven brass candlesticks with their chains, eighty-two women's garments, thirty-eight veils, sixteen men's garments, thirteen pair of men's shoes, forty-seven pair of women's shoes, eighteen cloaks . . .

After the cupboards and bookcases had been found to be empty, Silvanus (one of the subdeacons) brought forth a silver casket and a silver candlestick which he said he had found hidden behind a jug.

Victor of Aufidus (the police inspector) said to Silvanus, 'If you hadn't found these things, you would be a dead man.'

1. From St. Optatus, *Gesta apud Zenophilum*.

The search continued from room to room, with Felix, the perpetual flamen and curator, continually demanding that the Christians produce their copies of the Scriptures. Eventually they produced one 'very large codex', protesting that the Readers had the others. When Felix asked where these Readers lived, the two subdeacons Catullinus and Marcuclius said they didn't know. 'If you don't know where they are living, tell us their names,' Felix said.

Catullinus and Marcuclius said, 'We are not traitors. Here we are. Kill us if you want to.'

The two subdeacons were thereupon arrested, and the search party went to the homes of the Readers, some of whom had already run away, leaving their wives to confront the perpetual flamen and his investigators. Apparently these poor frightened people eventually surrendered all their precious books and so saved their lives; but by doing so, they left a legacy of suspicion and hatred which divided the African Church for the remainder of its history. For the controversy concerning Bishop Paul, his deacons, subdeacons, and grave-diggers continued for the next 400 years, with both factions, that is, the Catholics and the Donatists, accusing the other of betraying the faith. One can see from the original reports which are almost the prototypes of comparable investigations recently made into subversive organisations and individuals that the ultimate moral issue is not the surrendering of the books, chalices, chafing vessels, lamps, candlesticks, and the rest, but the betrayal of friends and colleagues. Hence the reiterated demand of the perpetual flamen and curator, 'Tell us their names!' and the brave reply of the two subdeacons, 'We are not traitors'.

We know from this and similar reports that thousands of early Christians were prepared to suffer and even die for their faith and that it was their fervour which finally defeated the whole vast apparatus of the pagan world. But victory was not won before hundreds of martyrs were butchered in the arena and thousands of ordinary Christians were sent to the mines, imprisoned, fined, or harassed by some regulation or the other. In the final days of the persecutions, when the old order fought its last battle with the new dispensation, no one could escape, for all Christian bishops and priests were ordered to be exiled; Christian associations were pronounced illegal; visits and reunions in Christian cemeteries were prohibited; and those who refused to comply were either executed or condemned to forced labour. In short, Christians were now outside the law and, as 'criminals', were subjected to the punishments reserved for the most heinous offenders, like parricides and assassins. They were frequently condemned *ad bestias* or *ad metalla*, the one meaning death in the arena, the other servitude in the mines.

As we have seen in the case of the Zliten mosaic which depicted two presumed Garamantes being torn to pieces by leopards, the inhuman practice known as *datio ad bestias* took place regularly in the amphitheatres all over the Roman world, so that during the worst days of the persecution every one of these vast structures must have been the scene of the death of thousands of Christians. It is obvious that this brutal spectacle was the most popular of the public entertainments, in which every tyrant strove to excel his predecessor. The excitement, of course, was not limited to the killing of human beings, whether gladiators or prisoners, but also included the exhibition of a veritable zoo of wild animals—lions, tigers, elephants, giraffes, wild boar, deer, and gazelle all on show together, the object being to watch them hunt and kill one another. Under these conditions the animals were usually too frightened and bewildered to oblige the spectators, whence the practice of throwing human victims to the more savage creatures, which even then had to be goaded into attacking their prey. For these beasts were instinctively wary of human beings, whether the latter were sent into the arena unfettered or were bound to a stake as bait.

Many legends have originated from undoubtedly real life episodes arising from the reluctance of lions in particular to maul helpless Christians—though not perhaps on the account of the martyr's religion. Of these myths that of Androcles is best known, though this African slave is not a subject of Christian hagiography. St. Marciana, however, is, for she was martyred in the arena at Caesarea, today a small coastal village called Cherchel, seventy-five miles west of Algiers. It is recalled of this Christian virgin that she was first imprisoned, tortured, and presented to the gladiators for their pleasure. Her biographer reports that she miraculously escaped being sullied by these hired killers, though the modern commentator might prefer to credit these slaves—victims, like the girl, of the system—with sentiments of decency and even pity. At all events, we are told that the audience in the amphitheatre began to shout for Marciana to be thrown to the wild beasts, whereupon she was brought in and tied to a stake—the usual procedure. At this point, a lion was sent into the arena. The beast came up to the girl, stood in front of her, then, placing his paws on her breast, sniffed her, and, 'smelling the odour of sanctity', left her and slunk away. There is no reason to disbelieve this story, or its sequel, which relates that a bull which was introduced next into the ring gored her, after which she was torn to pieces by a leopard which had replaced the lion. The bull, tormented by goading, might well have swung at the girl with his horns, and the leopard, smelling blood, would then attack her.

The most pitiable account of an animal's 'recognition' of a Christian martyr is that of the Passion of St. Thecla of Palestine, condemned to death during the great persecutions of A.D. 304–05. This girl was first stripped naked, then thrust into the arena to face the lions and bears which had been turned loose therein. Thereupon a lioness ran towards her and lay down at her feet, which it licked very gently. When a bear ambled close, the lioness sprang on it and tore it to pieces. Next a lion which had been trained to eat human flesh was sent into the arena. The lioness at once attacked the lion and the two animals fought until they killed each other. Now, without a lioness to protect her, Thecla was finally mauled to death by other animals, making no effort to save herself, but standing in the centre of the ring with her hands raised to heaven in the *orante* attitude of the early Christians when they prayed.

The early writers and, later, Christian tradition have rightly considered martyrdom in the Roman amphitheatres as the ultimate justification of their spiritual and moral crusade, for it was certainly Christians who roused the conscience of the world to the horrors and bestiality of the games. Their argument was that 'there is no difference between watching a murder and committing it'. It is true that nearly all cultivated pagans would have agreed with them in condemning gladiatorial combats and the other forms of cold-blooded murder which constituted the day's sport in the arena. But none of them, neither philosophers nor rulers, really ever did anything concrete to prohibit these spectacles, or even to humanise them. The plain fact was that the passion of the mob for the games was so fierce that no one dared interdict them, and for even an emperor to have tried to do so would have been tantamount to a modern ruler attempting to proscribe football or boxing. The games, religious in origin (and going back, of course, to the cult of human sacrifice), were sacrosanct from the point of view of pagan society. In fact, they continued long after Christianity became the official religion of the Empire.

Posterity, then, can thank Christian writers like Tertullian, Augustine, Eusebius, and others for the final abolition of horrors like the *datio ad bestias*, which in the latter days of the pagan empire had reached the point where women condemned for adultery were used as *pilae*, or dummies, in the arenas: that is, thrown into the ring, often naked, to be tossed by a bull in order to excite the animal before its combat with a bullfighter. Christian women, many of them virgins, were frequently abused in this manner, if we are to believe the reports of the early Christian historians.

The crusade of the early Fathers against another institution of the pagan world was less successful: this was the condemnation *ad metalla*, or prison sentence in the mines. It was the most dreaded of all punishments after the *datio ad bestias*, which, though meaning certain death, was preferable to some to the prolonged ordeal of the mines. The punishment *ad metalla*, in fact, was originally reserved for criminals like bandits, tomb-robbers, and the profaners of temples. It was reckoned so harsh that the sentence was limited to ten years, though a prisoner's chances of surviving that long, in view of the excessive brutality of the guards, were slim. Thus the Christians condemned to the mines under the Edicts of Valerian and Decius were first whipped, then branded on the forehead with a red-hot iron, and finally shackled—the chain passing between the ankles and so up to the waist by a short length. Escape under these conditions was impossible. In some cases, notably in Palestine, where the régime was most brutal, prisoners were mutilated in an outrageous manner—castrated, hamstrung, blinded in one eye, and the socket cauterised with a red-hot iron.

The long columns marching to the mines consisted of men, women, and children and all were thrown into pits and caves together, where many promptly died after their sufferings on the road. The rest were given a piece of bread once a day, no clothes, no sleeping facilities, no means of washing themselves, and no opportunity of celebrating mass. A contemporary record describes the conditions in the mines:

> Many [writes Diodorus of Sicily] die of their sufferings. They have no rest and live the most miserable life. Physical strength and the will to live enable a few to survive for a time, but death under these conditions is preferable to a life of continual work, night and day, with no possibility of escape. The guards consist of soldiers recruited from the barbarians who speak an incomprehensible jargon, making it impossible to bribe them for love or money.

If we consider the quantity of marble used throughout the Roman dominions during almost a thousand years of empire we can obtain some idea of the enormous production of the stone and the vast numbers of labourers required to mine it. All these workers were either slaves, prisoners-of-war, or condemned criminals, and serving with them were tens of thousands of Christians working the quarries of Europe, Asia, and Africa. The African mines became one of the main sources of supply, and some of them which had been worked by the Carthaginians and throughout the Roman occupation are still in operation today. Such are the marble quarries in the mountains near the Algerian-Tunisian border, at a place called Chemtou, or, in its Roman form, Simittu. These particular mines yielded the much-prized Numidian marble which is found in many of the Roman monuments of Italy as well as in those of the rich North African cities.

Simittu, in fact, became the headquarters of the African marble industry from the first to the sixth century and, as a result, grew into a city of considerable size and importance. The numerous population was supplied by an aqueduct which brought water from a spring fifteen miles away, and the city could boast of imposing public baths, an amphitheatre, and the usual temples, triumphal arches, and roads of a rich Afro-Roman settlement. Just outside the town in the surrounding hills are found the famous quarries which belong, like the amphitheatres, to early Christian history. The place almost tells its own story without the aid of written records, for the hillsides are still littered with blocks of marble exactly as they were left by the miners. The Roman passion for efficiency enables us to identify some of these blocks, for they are stamped with the date that they were hewn from the quarry, the name of the overseer, and their serial number. Thus, we can say that such and such a slab of marble was mined at Simittu in A.D. 107 during the reign of Trajan; its production was supervised by an overseer named Teseus; and it was the 562nd block quarried that year.[1]

Conditions in the slave camps attached to the mines were appalling, as the contemporary records prove, for as long as the imperial administration had an inexhaustible supply of forced labour, those condemned *ad metalla* were regarded as expendable. The only comparable prisons are the concentration camps of recent history in which the inmates were either worked or starved to death. Yet even under these conditions, some Christians managed to retain their faith and even to worship together at their homemade altars; for if the explorer penetrates into one of the huge man-made caverns

1. See Inscription No. 18 reported in 'Les Inscriptions de Chemtou', *Revue Archéologique*, July 1881, p. 32.

where the miners followed a vein of marble, he will come across visible proof of the Christians' presence. Little bands of the faithful had found the time and opportunity, no doubt during the absence of the overseer, to make shrines at a spot which they had to pass every day as they marched into the bowels of the mountain. One suddenly comes across the telltale Chi-Rho monogram enclosed in a circle and engraved into the rock with this inscription:

OFFINVT

NTAADIO

TIMO

VG ☧ NL

INRI

DIBUS

There is, then, no mistaking the monogram of Christ, or the formula I N R I, though the inscription itself is not at all clear. A French epigraphist gives the sense as 'This shrine was made by Diotimus, our freedman. . . .'

By a strange coincidence of history, we know, in addition to existence of this Diotimus, the names of a number of Christian leaders who worked, and no doubt died, in the same mines at Simittu during the second half of the third century, for St. Cyprian, the Bishop of Carthage, addresses them in one of his letters:

> Nemesianus, Felix, Lucius, another Felix, Litteus, Polianus, Victor, Jader, Dativus, and all the other faithful who, in the mines, testify to God the Father and to Jesus Christ our Lord and our Protector . . .

> O very valiant and very faithful soldiers of Christ, you have put into deeds what before you were taught in words; and since your prayers are now efficacious, pray that we, too, will be found worthy to achieve martyrdom.[1]

Cyprian was, of course, found worthy, and he died with great courage and dignity on an autumn day in A.D. 258, convinced that he would meet his fellow Christians who had been martyred in the mines or the amphitheatres in a happier and more beautiful world.

1. St. Cyprian, Letters, No. 76.

12 *Triumph and Defeat*

Christianity eventually triumphed over paganism at the beginning of the fourth century, to become the official religion of the Roman Empire. It was nowhere as flourishing as in Africa, where over 2,000 Christian communities have been identified and the names of 1,500 bishops, priests, deacons, and others have been traced in documents and epitaphs. But these figures are undoubtedly incomplete, since a thorough archaeological survey has never been made, and all that the French historians could do during their occupation of the North African territories was to identify the more obvious churches, chapels, monasteries, cemeteries, tombs, and inscriptions which have survived above ground. How much evidence remains hidden, it is impossible to say, and we may never know the full story of either the extent to which the Berber people were whole-hearted members of the Church, or why they abandoned their faith so completely. Yet remote oases on the edge of vast sand seas testify to the size of their Christian communities whose bishops attended the ecumenical councils at Carthage, and did so until as late as A.D. 484. One example of such an oasis, which the tourist can reach today without difficulty or discomfort, is Tozeur on the Chott Djerid in southern Tunisia, a picturesque village of date palms, mud-brick houses, and a Europeanised hotel from which the visitor can set out on a docile camel to tour the palmery, probably not realising that this typical Saharan oasis was in Roman times a Christian centre which could boast a basilica ornamented in the cloister style with rows of marble columns. Asellicus, the bishop of Tozeur, in fact, was in correspondence with St. Augustine himself; yet today there will not be found a single native Christian, though there is a Jewish community, which is curious, since Augustine's letter to Asellicus concerns the controversy as to who were the true Israelites, the actual Jews or the Christians. Augustine maintained the latter in his 196th Letter to the Bishop and congregation of Tozeur who seemed to have been on the point of embracing Judaism, and may actually have done so, explaining the presence of the Jews in this orthodox Moslem region.

The ruins visible above ground are only a part of the story of Christian Africa. The underground cities of the dead are even more evocative of that lost world. How many of these catacombs there were in Africa is unknown, and will remain so unless they are discovered accidentally. For by the twelfth century the location of even the catacombs of Rome was forgotten, with the exception of those attached to the Church of St. Sebastian on the Appian Way; and it has been largely by accident that the 800 miles and the estimated 2,000,000 graves of the Italian secret cemeteries have been discovered at all. In the same manner, the finding of the mile-long catacombs of Sousse in Tunisia was the result of pure chance. A French officer who was strolling around noticed a hole in the ground, thrust in his cane and, finding only empty space, decided forthwith to excavate. Within a few hours his gang of native workmen had broken through the roof of a tunnel into the catacombs of the Good Shepherd, one of the great historical finds of North Africa. Yet whether the Sousse catacombs were unique is still uncertain, though it must be considered highly unlikely. This particular Tunisian town, the Colonia Ulpia Trajana Augusta Frugifera Hadrumetina of the Romans and the Justinianapolis of the Byzantines, was a comparatively small and unimportant community in comparison with Carthage, for instance; and the supposition must be that if Sousse had over a mile of catacombs where 10,000 Christians were interred, the larger cities of Roman Africa must have had similar underground cemeteries. In fact, seven other sites have been reported by travellers, though unfortunately they seldom give us adequate information as to their exact location.

For this reason, my wanderings in search of what sounded like a particularly interesting Christian necropolis were fruitless. The catacombs I was looking for were reported to be under a church near the Algerian town of Khenchela, thirty-five miles south-east of Constantine, in the foothills of the Aurès Mountains. Khenchela, once a provincial Roman city called Mascula, is reached across a wide marshy plain strewn with monuments, indicating that this region was one of the most prosperous departments of Roman Africa. Today this country is occupied by a few peasant farmers with their flocks, and despite the ruins of the fortresses, cities, and villas of the old civilisation, there is little to show that this region was a Christian land with numerous churches, shrines, and cemeteries.

The catacombs I had come to see were said to be under a church 'on a little hill on Khenchela–Babar road'. The report by the Abbé Leynaud of the White Fathers stated:

> Here can be seen the ruins of an important basilica under which lie the catacombs. The entry had been closed by a flagstone set in a frame of dressed stone. It recalled the entry into the Roman catacombs. About eight feet under this flagstone (which is well below the level of the soil), there is a circular gallery of quite a large size with other tunnels branching off. In the walls of the galleries, tiers of *loculi* (i.e., niches in the rock for the entombment of the dead) have been cut and sealed off with mud bricks. Many of these *loculi* are open, the humidity having disintegrated the bricks (which were made of mud and baked in the sun), and the bodies which lay inside could be seen.
>
> Unfortunately, further examination of these catacombs couldn't be undertaken, even though they might have yielded valuable information and, probably, Christian epitaphs of the greatest interest. Caving-in of the tunnels made digging difficult but we haven't given up hope of undertaking the work one day. . . .[1]

This fascinating monument was unknown to my guide,

1. Abbé A.-F. Leynaud, *Les Catacombes Africaines*, pp. 350–1.

though he was himself an amateur archaeologist and had dug around in the ruined Byzantine city of Baghai, famous as the capital of the Donatist sect. He had, in fact, unearthed a large commemorative slab dedicated to the Emperor Justinian and his consort Theodora, the little mime and prostitute who became empress of the Roman world in A.D. 527. But of the church on the Khenchela–Babar road he knew nothing; nor did the farmers and shepherds who occupied huts partially built from the rubble of the Roman villas. In short, we did not find Abbé Leynaud's reported catacombs, so 'the valuable information and Christian epitaphs of the greatest interest' still lie under the ground, unrecorded.

One hopes that the archaeologists will one day find and explore this site for often the catacombs are the only cemeteries of antiquity which have not been plundered, either because their entrance was well hidden, or because the tomb-robbers feared to get lost in these underground warrens. Even the police sent to arrest Christian fugitives used to hesitate to go further into the maze than they had to and in the celebrated case of the martyrs Chrysanthus and Daria[1] simply executed their orders by walling up the two Christians and their followers in a chapel just inside the entrance of the catacomb of Thraso in Rome. The scene of their martyrdom was for a long time a shrine for pilgrims who were able to look through a grill in the wall and see the bones of the immured saints.

By their very nature, then, the catacombs were the headquarters of the Christians during their long war with the pagan authorities. Inside these subterranean cities the faithful could assemble and conduct their forbidden rites with some safety. Inside were the little chapels dedicated to the martyrs. And along the walls of the tunnels were excavated the niches where the devout could be buried in sanctified ground.

We see by comparing the catacombs of Italy with those in Roman provinces like Africa that the constructions of these quasi-secret refuges followed a simple pattern. The necropolis

1. This Roman lady was said to have been a Vestal Virgin to whom Chrysanthus was married in what ecclesiastical historians refer to as 'a virginal matrimonial union'.

had a single entry which led by a steep flight of steps down to the main tunnel. This shaft was driven through the rock just high and wide enough to allow two grave-diggers to hack out niches in either wall. The niches were cut long enough to fit the corpse, large for adults and small for children. The dead were placed in their grave wrapped in their winding sheet and then walled up with rubble and cement. The tombs of the richer or more important deceased were marked by a mosaic plaque on which was inscribed their name and virtues, together with the favourite Christian symbols—the peacock, dove, fish, lamp. The less affluent were memorialised by a simple tile or fragment of marble on which their name was scratched with the valediction IN PACE. Scores of these early Christians' names testify to the extent to which the Berber Africans had embraced the new religion—names like Passibal, Brumasa, Nilles, Serot, Akuzr. Occasionally the phrase IN PACE is replaced by the more militant VINCE, the two formulas both implying that the African Christian in those early days was engaged throughout his lifetime in a continuous battle for survival.

Yet despite the ultimate victory of the Christian cause throughout the Roman world, the African Church, built up over seven centuries, was overthrown within a few decades by the new religion of Islam. The proud claim of Tertullian that the Church of Christ was invincible was not proven true in Africa. To the contrary, this region of the continent was to become an implacable enemy of Christianity and has always been indifferent, if not outright hostile, to all attempts to re-introduce the old faith. Mohammed has triumphed so completely over Jesus among the Berber Moslems that most ecclesiastical authorities are forced, however reluctantly, to concede that there is no longer much point in continuing their evangelisation. Some of the reasons for this failure to persuade Moslems to apostatise are self-obvious. To a people dwelling in a poor and arid country, the emphasis which Christianity places upon suffering and self-denial is counter to their very instincts; while, conversely, the promise of a Paradise in which the deficiencies of nature will be compensated for by the delights of unlimited physical indulgence is the most attractive reward religion can offer to simple men. Islam offers the desert-dweller to whom thirst is a continual ordeal perpetual springs of sweet water, fresh fruit, and cool breezes. Moreover, Mohammedanism is based on a realistic moral code which does not make unnatural demands on the spiritual or physical capabilities of the practitioner. The Christian ambivalence on the matter of sexual gratification, for instance, is not a dilemma to the Moslem, while the rules concerning good conduct, even in specific cases such as the giving of alms, are laid down clearly and simply, which is not the case in Christian dogma.

Secondly, the Prophet's rationalisation of polygamy was a practical solution of a complex social and moral problem. We note that polygamy, or to be more precise, polygyny in the sense of a plurality of concubines, was a basic institution of both the pagan and early Christian worlds, even though it was severely condemned by the sterner Christian moralists from the time of St. Paul onwards. The resultant confusion between theory and practice was one more example of the dissensions which divided the Christian world. For despite the strict views on chastity advocated by the apologists, the lay Christian continued to hold pagan attitudes about love and marriage. Indeed, the persistence of profligacy was undoubtedly the reason why the more fervent leaders of the early Church, indignant at the foul charges levelled against them by their adversaries, went so far as to prove their continence by castrating themselves. The great Origen himself was one such, while other holy men willingly underwent the same mutilation, despite the disapproval of both State and Church. As late as A.D. 489, we hear of a church dignitary called Acacus who, having been accused by the bishops of fornication, demanded that his detractors have visual proof of his innocence.

No such questionings or doubts about the rightness of sexual pleasure troubled the Moslem, so that we may assume that the African of the eighth century, fervent Christian though he might have been, was glad to have the sin of venery off his conscience. As for pagan Africa, nearly all observers agree that polygamy is not a manifestation of sexual indulgence, but a necessity in societies where women have no rights and no protection other than matrimony. The Moslem laws regarding both multiple marriages and concubinage give women the protection they receive from no other quarter; whence all African travellers, with the exception of the missionaries, agree that women's lives would be intolerable in the rural communities were it not for polygamy. Polygamy ensures that the menial tasks (never performed by the husband) are shared by other wives; and, above all, that each woman has a period of respite before and after pregnancy. The arguments in favour of the system can go farther than this, for socially the institution ensures the advantages of marriage and motherhood to practically all women, irrespective of their physical attractiveness; and morally it eliminates the basic causes of prostitution.

Thirdly (still examining the reasons for the triumph of Islam over Christianity), every follower of Mohammed was a missionary for the new faith in that he practised and demonstrated his faith in public, several times a day, whereas Christian ritual was more and more confined to priests and special occasions, with the layman playing a passive rôle in his devotions. Public worship five times a day, performed, for instance, by caravans crossing the desert, creates a sense of genuine brotherhood which was, originally, a strong bond between Christians. Moreover, this brotherhood born of communal rites performed in the open air undoubtedly transcends differences in race, colour, and even social position, so that it is not surprising that miscegenation is no general problem in Moslem countries. Africans, very conscious that white is the colour of purity in Christian doctrine, black the colour of the Devil, found, and find, no such psychological discrimination in Mohammedanism.

13 *The Return of the Christians*

Against this powerful appeal of Islam, Christianity was to have very little success for the next thousand years and more. 'The Moslem is so sure of the superiority of his religion', a Christian scholar writes in this century, 'that attempts to convert him appear to be all but hopeless.'[1] Some 250 years earlier, describing missionary work among the Africans, the Capuchin missionary, Father Zucchelli, reported that 'the pagans are, in fact, nothing else than baptised heathen who have no Christianity about them but the bare name'.

These are conclusions that theologians and missionaries were forced to accept until quite recently, though the issue tends to become obscured by the misuse of statistics. But not even statistics can hide the fact that Christianity has been rejected by Moslems, and the explanation is not far to seek. The Moslem and the Christian worlds were at war from the middle of the seventh until the end of the nineteenth century. To the Christians, the Arab invasions of Africa and southern Europe were terrible calamities; and to the Moslems, the Christian wars against them, including the Crusades, were regarded in the same manner. The fact that Christian priests held crosses aloft during the attack on Jerusalem in 1099, for instance, did not impress the besieged Mohammedans with the spiritual zeal as much as with the ferocity of the soldiers, who put all the population to the sword, regardless of sex or age. In short, twelve centuries of wars between the adherents of the two religions resulted in very few conversions indeed, but ended, rather, in a legacy of hatred and suspicion.

1. Dr. Diedrich Westermann, *Africa and Christianity*, 1937, p. 122.

It is understandable, then, that the first missionaries to Moslem Africa were not regarded as men of God who came in goodwill. Rather, they were only tolerated as brokers engaged in the business of ransoming Christian prisoners-of-war. A few attempted to convert the infidel, usually with meagre, if not disastrous, results. Indeed, one of the first met his death at the hands of the mob, and we see in his activities and methods the almost hopeless nature of the enterprise. The missionary in question was Ramon Lull, a philosopher, poet, theologian, and mystic who was called the 'illuminated doctor'. Born on the island of Majorca about 1234, he became a hermit at the age of thirty and was suddenly inspired with a burning desire to convert the Moslems of North Africa. For this purpose he devoted himself to the Arabic language and philosophy, and in order to present the Christian faith in such a manner that even the infidel could not fail to see the truth, he invented a machine which by means of levers, cogs, and cranks always came up with the proof of his Christian propositions, or answers to difficult theological questions. This machine tackled such conundrums as 'Could God be God if he could sin?' 'Do the devils desire to die?' 'What language do the angels speak?' and 'Is a poor man more capable of giving true testimony than a rich woman?'

Evidently this machine was too cumbersome to take with him when Ramon first went to Tunis at about the age of sixty. But as an Arabic scholar, he was permitted to dispute religion and philosophy with his hosts, since Moslems have always had a great regard, amounting almost to reverence, for learned men. But he always began and ended his dissertations with the categorical statement that 'the law of the Christians is holy and true, and the creed of the Moslems is false and wrong;' and this proposition was flatly rejected by his intelligent listeners and met with a shower of stones by the unintelligent. It was during one of these attacks that he met his death in Tunis at the age of eighty—in a manner reminiscent of his youthful prayer, 'Thy servant and Thy subject, O Lord, has a very great fear of dying a natural death . . . for he would fain have his death the noblest that is—namely, death for Thy love'.

For the next three centuries, the task of converting the North Africans was left to Franciscan and Dominican monks who frequently met with martyrdom without making any visible impression on the minds of the infidel. In fact, no concerted attempts at all were made to evangelise North Africa until the European conquests of the nineteenth century. Instead, the Church's attention was turned to pagan Africa, where the Portuguese, under the direction of Prince Henry the Navigator (1390–1460), were exploring the coasts of the Dark Continent.

There were difficulties. The ships' captains whom Henry engaged to sail south from the home base at Lagos (Portugal) were loathe to go beyond Cape Bojador, latitude 26°, in the belief that any Christian so doing would be at once changed into a Negro. Further, there was the evidence of Arab writers that the waters of the Atlantic below Bojador were actually on the boil, whence any mariner venturing that far would be cooked inside his vessel. None the less, bold men were commissioned by Prince Henry to press on farther and farther south, not only with the intention of exploration but also of 'destroying the Moors and exalting the Catholic faith'.

In the final years of the fifteenth century the Portuguese achieved a brilliant success, for by 1498 Vasco da Gama had rounded the Cape of Good Hope and crossed the Indian Ocean to reach India itself. The 'exaltation of the Catholic faith', granted to the explorers in a papal Letter of Indulgence, was likewise achieved; for the African kings of those lands visited or conquered by the Portugese men-of-war regarded the white men and their powerful God with considerable awe. Conversions, therefore, were relatively easy and certainly rapid where material aid in the form of European contrivances was forthcoming. In 1491 we hear of the king of the Congo and his chief wife being baptised and given the god-names of the reigning king and queen of Portugal. Further, the African capital was renamed San Salvador, a church was built, and a mission of Portuguese friars sent out to administer to the spiritual welfare of the new flock. A hundred years or so later, Spanish conquistadores had a similar success with the king of Sierra Leone, who was converted and agreed to divorce all his wives save one, though there were complications when the queen refused baptism on the grounds that she feared the white man's magic. She was, however, sprinkled with holy water; the king assumed the name of Philip after the Spanish monarch; and since all his family and subjects automatically adopted the new religion, the Church was strengthened overnight by the addition of several hundred thousand African converts.

A characteristic reminder of these first attempts to Christianise Africa is seen in the magnificent Portuguese sea-castle on the Atlantic coast of Morocco at a place formerly called Mazagan, now known as El Jadida. Here the Portuguese built a citadel in 1502, which became a fortress-city, housing a garrison of 2,000 soldiers and 1,000 civilians. In the west the city faced the Atlantic Ocean whose tides washed against the enormous walls; on the other three sides it was defended by towers and turrets in the manner of a medieval castle. It was, for those days, impregnable. Inside stood the parish church of our Lady of the Assumption, today partially restored and used for the odds and ends of artifacts found in the district—two old Portuguese cannon lying in the nave, some cannon balls, and a slab of stone whose inscription one is unable to read because of the absence of light. The interior is simple, with a balcony at one end and inscriptions on the walls recording the foundation of the church and its various chapels built by the sixteenth-century captains of the fort. Nearby is the citadel proper, which comprises the governor's chapel and palace, a hospital, prison, and the famous *salle d'armes*, today called 'the Cistern'—surely the most beautiful Gothic structure in Africa, an underground cathedral whose massive pillars, twenty-five in number, arch up into fan-shaped vaults. Water dripping from the roof covers the red brick floor and makes a still lake in which the roof is reflected in the light of lanterns. At midday, the sun shines through a circular opening in the roof on to the central fountain. This great underground chamber served as a mustering ground of the Portuguese soldiers, a warehouse, cistern, and finally a Moroccan *bagnio*, or underground prison for slaves, including Christians captured from the southern coasts of England and Ireland by the Moorish pirates.

All that is now left of the Christians in Mazagan is a little ornate chapel of the Spanish friars of St. Vincent de Paul, the Christian slave who was imprisoned in 'the Cistern'. Otherwise this seaport, once considered the best harbour along the West African coast, exists only as a tourist resort. Its only maritime activity, despite the jetties and quays left by the French for a fishing fleet which is no longer active, seems to consist of attempts to repair a few old hulks left stranded in the canal. Yet to maintain this outpost of their new empire the Portuguese galleons must have been constantly coming and going with replacements and supplies for the garrison of 3,000 men—a succession of governors, captains, soldiers, and priests who held this fortress for 250 years in the name of the king and the Holy Catholic Church.

The last Portuguese ship called in at Mazagan in 1769, with orders to evacuate. The garrison thereupon burnt their houses and furniture, killed their horses, and left, as a farewell gift, a delayed-action mine which killed numbers of the Moroccan besiegers when they entered the citadel. Thus ended the Portuguese empire in Morocco and, with it, the high hopes of converting the infidel.

But while their missionary priests had little success with the Moslems, they could count their pagan converts by the tens of thousands—1,500 Congolese being baptised by a Jesuit during one short tour through the jungle, for instance. Perhaps many of these Africans would have remained Christians if their temporal and spiritual masters had not fallen out over the division of territory, and it is conceivable that the Congo would have developed from the feudal society which the Portuguese imposed on it, by creating Negro dukes, lords, marquises, and the lower orders in the European manner. But once the military units with their accompanying priests were driven out by rival colonists, the Africans relapsed into their old ways, and all that was left of the fifteenth- and sixteenth-century missions when the next wave of missionaries arrived in the mid-nineteenth century were the ruins of Christian churches and sundry artifacts used by the witch-doctors as ju-jus. The *santu* (from *santa cruz*) or wooden crosses left behind by the Portuguese priests were still considered powerful charms for hunting, no doubt because of their association with the white man's blunderbusses.

> When we reached San Salvador in 1879 [W. H. Bentley the Baptist missionary writes] it was to all intents and purposes a heathen land . . . In a house in the king's compound were kept a large crucifix and some images of saints, but they were only the king's fetishes. If the rains were insufficient, they were sometimes brought out and carried round the town . . . Old crucifixes are to be found among the insignia of some chiefs; and now and then a Portuguese missal. . . .[1]

The first phase of the modern evangelisation of Africa, then, began about A.D. 1500, when the Portuguese set up trading stations around the coast, and, mindful of their obligations to the Church, nearly always included priests in their expeditions. A report of 1505 describes the method of occupation: 'Upon landing, the friars set up a cross before which the canticle *Te Deum Laudamus* was chanted, and when this was completed, the place was given up to plunder.' Part of the plunder in such cases was invariably a consignment of Negroes who were shipped back to Lisbon, together with other merchandise; and in order to dispose of the prisoners, markets were set up in the Portuguese ports. The first of these, founded at Lisbon with the approval of the Pope in 1537, was the prototype of the European slave markets.

It would be wholly unjustified to assert that the Portuguese,

1. W. H. Bentley, *Pioneering in the Congo*, Vol. I, pp. 35–6.

or any other European nation, were the innovators of this infamous trade. To the contrary, as we shall see in the next chapter, slavery has always been endemic to Africa, so that the Negro captives of the white men could not have envisaged any fate other than death or enslavement. The Negroes themselves, in other words, had no experience and hence no concept of mercy in the Christian sense; and the moral implications of treating human beings like cattle troubled the white captors more than their black captives, especially the Christian missionaries and all humanitarians. The dismay of the evangelists is best summed up by the Jesuit priest Father Barrosa, who worked in the Congo from 1881 to 1887:

> The Negro saw, and compared with his rude intelligence, the teaching and the works. They did not coincide. While the Christian missionary proclaimed the lofty dignity of the child of God by grace, the Christian trader counted one more 'piece' (*peça*: i.e., slave) for his gang.

But objections to the slave trade on the part of the Church came later, towards the end of the eighteenth century. Before this crisis of conscience the commerce was not confined to laymen. Thus, a Jesuit monastery at Luanda in Angola possessed 12,000 slaves; and when the trade was at its height between Angola and Brazil (nearly 10,000 slaves a year being shipped out of the Portuguese colony) the Bishop of Luanda was regularly carried on his episcopal chair to the quayside in order to bless the ships and crews and to exhort the cargo to accept baptism and the Christian religion.

After centuries of mistreatment it was inevitable that Africans should regard the white man and his God with fear and suspicion, so that during the second phase of evangelisation in the nineteenth century Christian missionaries had considerable difficulty in obtaining the natives' confidence. The braver and more zealous of the gospellers who penetrated into the still-uncharted interior were often forced to defend themselves with firearms against attacks from hostile tribes; and even after they had obtained a foothold in unfriendly territory were liable to see several years of devoted work destroyed overnight by a sudden explosion of hate and suspicion. Indeed, the long story of their tribulations does not end with the dangers they encountered in the field, for the record of missionary endeavour in Africa is further darkened by dissensions between and within the Christian sects themselves.

The experience of the Dutch missionary George Schmidt is not untypical. Schmidt chose as his territory a Hottentot region known as the Valley of the Baboons. After he had set up his mission station, he was faced with the problem of the Hottentot language which no European had yet succeeded in mastering. This curious tongue had been accurately described by one of the first Europeans ever to hear it, namely the Elizabethan traveller Sir James Lancaster, who sums it up in these words:

> Their speech is wholly uttered through their throat, and they clocke with their tongue in such a sorte that even in seven weekes that we remained heere in this place, the sharpest wit among us could not learne one worde of their language.[1]

Despite his long sojourn among the Hottentots, George Schmidt was never able to converse in the 'Click' language of these South Africans and finally decided to compromise by teaching his flock Dutch. Then, after what he considered an adequate course in that tongue, he proceeded to read them Zinzendorf's *Berlin Discourses* and his own theological lectures on the Epistle to the Romans. He records in his diary that he discerned signs of inattention in his congregation. Moreover, not only were the Hottentots growing restless, but so were the missionary's superiors in Cape Town, where the Dutch Reformed Church claimed the exclusive right of converting the heathen, whether Hottentot, Bushman, or Zulu. And when Schmidt continued to baptise his converts in the stream hard by his hut, the churchmen in Cape Town charged him with heresy and arranged to have him shipped back to Holland.

1. *The Voyages of Sir James Lancaster, Kt, to the East Indies* (Ed. Clements R. Markham, 1877), pp. 63–4.

Above: These mud-brick forts may have been built by the Garamantes to protect the caravan routes from Central Africa to the coast

Offering tables for food, wine, and oil were placed outside the Garamantian tombs

Left: Roman mosaics depicting an orchestra and scenes from the arena, including a Garamantian prisoner-of-war being torn to pieces by a leopard

Foot of page: The castle at Mazagan in Morocco, built 1502 by the Portuguese. The arch on the left is the sea-gate where the galleons were unloaded

Opposite (top): The ruins of a fifth-century Roman church at Thibilis in Algeria. There is a cross on the keystone above the portal

Opposite (foot): The church of SS. Paul and Stephen, built in 1951 by the French, is still another relic of Christianity in Africa

Above: The 'frozen' waterfall at Hamman Meskoutine, Algeria. 25,000 gallons of near-boiling water erupt from underground every minute

Opposite (top): The Roman city of Thurbursicum Numidarum which Saint Augustine visited to discuss the Donatist heresy with Bishop Fortunatus

Opposite (foot): A Berber shepherd boy grazes his flocks among the ruins of a Roman city. The surrounding countryside is now barren

The atrocities committed by the Moslems against their Christian slaves were used as propaganda in the long war between Christendom and

'In the slave markets the young women were marked down as the booty of the local monarch'

Islam, which began with the Crusades and only ended with the suppression of the Barbary pirates

The Mediterranean galleys relied on oars more than sails. The Turks used Christian slaves as oarsmen, the Christians used Turks

The Barbarossa brothers were pirates to the Christians, but admirals of the fleet to the Turks

Below: British officers summoned to a divan to discuss the ransom of captives with the Bey of Algiers

The opposition to George Schmidt's mission on the part of rival ecclesiasts was to become a familiar pattern of African evangelisation throughout the later years of the nineteenth and the early years of the twentieth centuries. The strongest rivalry, of course, was between the Catholic and Protestant missions; but even within the main sects themselves, antipathies were frequently violent. Jesuits, Dominicans, and Franciscans vied with each other, sometimes unscrupulously, in their zeal to save the black men's souls; in the Protestant camp, dozens of sects took to the field as representatives of particular dogmas rather than of a unified church. They were nearly all brave men, comparable with that band of explorers who had opened up the interior of Africa in the cause of science and commerce. And as with the explorers, the mortality among the missionaries was enormous, reaching one hundred per cent in the case of those who penetrated to Equatorial Africa, unless they came home before they succumbed to the 'fever'.

One of those who did survive was the Anglican missionary Thomas Thompson who went to the Gold Coast in 1751 and returned to England, broken in health, in 1756. During these five years the Reverend Thompson had endured the typical trials and tribulations of his calling, the worst of which was, perhaps, the cynicism of the Moslems, who objected to his attempts to convert them on the grounds of the chronic insobriety and lecherous behaviour of the Christian soldiers and merchants. Even the pagans would only agree to attend divine service provided they were promised a grog ration at its conclusion. Notwithstanding, the Reverend Thompson returned to a quiet vicarage in Kent still convinced that 'the People might be brought to the Christian faith, despite their prejudice against me'. Part of that prejudice might have arisen from the clergyman's support of the slave trade of which he wrote a defence entitled, *The African Trade for Negro Slaves shown to be consistent with the Principles of Humanity and the Laws of Revealed Religion.* His arguments, which he supported by copious references to the Old Testament, were based on two premises:

1. Slavery had its origin from a principle of humanity and aversion to shedding human blood.

2. The grand source whence the marts are supplied with Negroes is war, which is carried on and waged by the contending nations with as little slaughter as possible, it being the business of the field not to kill, but make captives. Slavery, therefore, does not accrue by might overcoming right; but by the fortune of war; and partly from national customs of equal authority with laws: as the selling of criminals and insolvent debtors.

But despite the early Christian justification of the slave trade, conversions among the Negro pagans increased as the memory of past wrongs was forgotten in the realisation of the benefits which European missionaries could bring to people who had no other hope of material progress. Schools, hospitals, clothes, food, and bibles were the gifts of twentieth-century Christianity to heathen Africa as the missionaries laboured by their works as well as their teachings to capture both the minds and souls of their primitive flock. Their degree of success is sometimes measured in numbers, though the statistics vary with the source or are even denied by rival organisations.

Two sets of figures may be compared in order to obtain some idea of the Christianisation of Africa and to deduce from the statistics one's own conclusions. The first figures (A) are based on a 1954 report; the second (B) on the 1957 returns.[1]

	A	B
Roman Catholics:	12,043,732	17,000,000
Protestants:	8,806,786	13,000,000
Orthodox and Coptic:	4,602,986	5,000,000
African sects:	1,089,479	1,000,000
Total	26,542,983	36,000,000

1. From C. P. Groves, *The Planting of Christianity in Africa*, 1958, Vol. IV, p. 324; and *The World Christian Handbook*, Statistical Section, 1962.

The estimated population of the Continent is 200,000,000, indicating, if these figures are correct, that over one in seven Africans is a Christian in Table A; and over one in five in Table B. Unfortunately the rival sects are unwilling to accept each other's claims, the Protestants in particular objecting to the Catholic contention that their rate of conversions in Central Africa has increased sixty-five times in the last half-century. But even whether he accepts these figures or not, the missionary himself will readily admit that it is all too easy for the unsophisticated African 'to fall in' and just as easy for him 'to fall out'.

Statistics apart, the problems of evangelisation in Africa today are more complex than ever before. The old dilemmas are more acute; new ones are emerging. In the old days of colonialism, the issue was clear-cut. Christianity was the only true religion; all the others, and particularly heathen cults, were false. Again, the black man had been conquered with the greatest of ease by the white man, whence the former was regarded as physically and mentally inferior to the latter. Consequently, the African had to accept the pre-eminence of the European's religion, along with his political administration. This attitude, as we have seen, was reduced to its simplest form by the Portuguese and Spanish priests who declared their subjects 'Christian' by the thousands, even when the Africans were being treated as subhuman by their lay masters.

What, in fact, simplified the task of the first missionaries was their complete disapproval of the primitive cultures which the Christine doctrine was intended to supplant. In fact, to the sixteenth-century priest, the African had no 'culture' at all: he was, by classical standards, a savage. It is only quite recently that sociologists have begun to realise that the way of life of uncivilised peoples has a rational basis; that customs which strike the modern city-dweller as grotesque or senseless are essential to the welfare of the tribe. Two of these customs—polygamy and witchcraft—are as fundamental in African rural society as monogomy and socialised medicine are in Europe, whence it follows that an attack on such institutions is liable seriously to dislocate the communities that rely on them. It is only now that sociologists are prepared to admit that polygamy is designed to ensure the welfare and security of the family. The missionaries, however, could not, and still cannot, accept this justification of a custom which has always been abhorrent to Christian dogma, though certain Christian sects, notably the Moravians, have compromised to the extent of baptising polygamists and their wives. But the majority of denominations are adamant in their opposition to multiple marriages on the grounds that they are contrary to the law of Christ. Unfortunately, the argument is unconvincing to the African, since it appears to be contradicted by other evidence of Christian doctrine, specifically that based on the Old Testament in which the examples of Abraham, Solomon, and the Hebrew patriarchs appear to justify the custom of concubinage in addition to multiple marriages.

The second obstacle which the missionary has had to overcome is the African's addiction to witchcraft, the very concept of which tends to alienate the scientifically educated and materialistically oriented European from primitive peoples. Yet the aversion to witchcraft springs from an ignorance of African mythology which is still responsible for certain sophisticated forms of witchcraft. Greek mythology, then, is both beautiful and symbolic; African witchcraft is merely comic melodrama acted out by savages in grotesque masks—an affair of 'mumbo-jumbo'. But this interpretation overlooks one very important fact: magic has always been a fundamental factor in religion. Thus, to the African, whether he lives in the desert or the jungle, trees, rivers, rocks, and the very air itself are full of spirits, and the forces of good and evil are continuously around him. He sees no other explanation of why one man should be spared and another destroyed in exactly the same place at the same time, as when lightning strikes a caravan or village; whereas the European city-dweller who scarcely ever sees any manifestations of nature apart from the weather is satisfied to accept 'coincidence' as an explanation, unless, in a more religious frame of mind, he refers all disasters to the 'Will of God'. The evidence of both natural and divine indifference to personal misfortunes—

man's hunger, cold, disease, and all the tribulations that are inflicted on him through no fault of his own—are always before the African's eyes, and the theory of coincidence or causation is simply not good enough for him. He turns, therefore, to the witch-doctor rather than the priest for help, for the former is more understanding of his bewilderment. Indeed, this bewilderment, to which the Christian religion offers no solution except still further submission to misfortune, explains the substratum of voodooism which underlies nearly all varieties of Negro Christianity, comparable, one can suppose, to the popularity of astrology, fortune-telling, and the like in white culture. In other words, while overtly professing the white man's creed, the African may still be tied to the animistic beliefs of his forefathers who, in a time of trouble, needed something more positive in the way of help than appeals to an unseen God. And until he accepts a scientific explanation of the universe in which God is an intellectualised concept and nature a complex of mechanical forces, he will continue to do so.

This dichotomy in his thinking is, of course, emphasised by the very obvious fact that the Christian God is the particular deity of the white race to which His Son belonged during His sojourn on earth. Hence it could have come as no particular surprise to Africans when the Dutch Reformed Churches advocated outright the policy of apartheid on biblical and theological grounds, since they were simply reasserting what had been said many times before: that the white man was superior culturally, intellectually, and now spiritually to the black man. The result was bound to be that both thoughtful and emotional Africans identified Christianity with certain discriminatory policies and practices which negated the 'brotherhood in Christ' doctrine of the missionaries. In short, apartheid, like the use of the atom bomb by a Christian nation against non-Christians and, before that, the enslavement of tens of millions of Africans by Christians, may foreshadow the third failure to establish Christianity in the world's largest continent. For, as we have seen, the first great attempt was defeated by the inability of the Christians to live together in peace; the second collapsed when the Church supported the slave trade; and the third is bound to fail if the Christian theory of the brotherhood of man excludes in practice those whose skin is not white.

BOOK FIVE

Slavery—Black and White

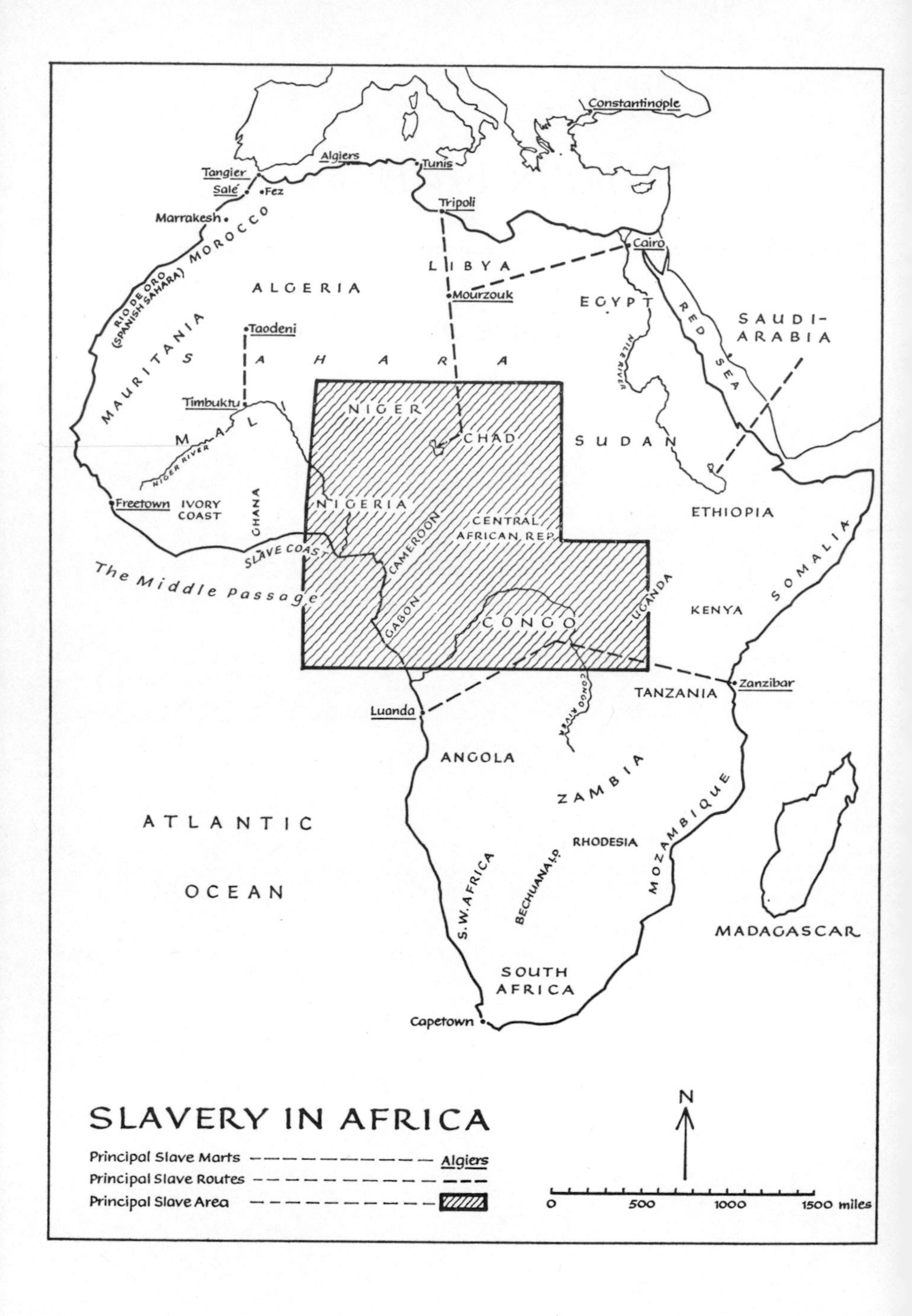

Constantinople
Algiers
Tunis
Tangier
Salé
Fez
Tripoli
Marrakesh
MOROCCO
Cairo
RIO DE ORO (SPANISH SAHARA)
LIBYA
ALGERIA
Mourzouk
EGYPT
RED SEA
SAUDI-ARABIA
MAURITANIA
Taodeni
NILE RIVER
SAHARA
Timbuktu
NIGER
MALI
CHAD
SUDAN
NIGER RIVER
Freetown
IVORY COAST
GHANA
NIGERIA
CENTRAL AFRICAN REP.
ETHIOPIA
CAMEROON
SLAVE COAST
SOMALIA
The Middle Passage
UGANDA
GABON
CONGO
KENYA
Zanzibar
TANZANIA
CONGO RIVER
Luanda
ANGOLA
ZAMBIA
MOZAMBIQUE
ATLANTIC
RHODESIA
BECHUANALD.
S.W. AFRICA
OCEAN
MADAGASCAR
SOUTH AFRICA
Capetown
SLAVERY IN AFRICA
N
Principal Slave Marts
Algiers
Principal Slave Routes
Principal Slave Area
0
500
1000
1500 miles

14 *African Slavery To-day*

The oasis of Mourzouk on the northern fringe of the Sahara Desert presents, in microcosm, still another lost African world—the world of the slave trade. Mourzouk somehow reeks of the misery of its inglorious past, symbolised by the huge, jerry-built Turkish citadel, the older and even more dilapidated Arab fort, and the adjacent market-place where the slaves were mustered after coming in from their two months' march across the desert. The town even has a third fort, a beautifully built Italian castle which exemplifies the highest standards of old-fashioned military architecture. Nothing like these desert forts will ever be built again, though their history goes back 2,000 years to a time when the Roman legions first erected them across the northern limits of the Sahara. But the fact that Mourzouk has three forts demonstrates its strategic importance in the old days of desert wars and the slave trade; and, by the same token, the air of decay which settles like the sand over forts, houses, and streets shows that both wars and trade have ceased.

The end as far as Mourzouk was concerned came less than forty years ago when the last-known slave caravan arrived here from Central Africa in 1929. Both the event and the date are significant, for they mark the finish of an era. They also mark the decline of Mourzouk from the capital of the Fezzan and the largest slave mart in the Sahara to a dying desert community which has scarcely any commerce at all with the outside world. For this oasis lived and flourished for centuries on a trade which involved the entire continent from the Mediterranean ports to the Cape of Good Hope, from the Atlantic coast to the Indian Ocean, affecting the lives of literally tens of millions of people of many nationalities. In fact, up to that year, 1929, when the last officially recorded caravan arrived, an estimated 100,000,000 Negroes had been taken out of Africa by Christian and Moslem slave traders during almost 500 continuous years of wars, manhunts, and forced marches; while, within the same period, tens of thousands of Christian slaves were making the journey the other way, captives of the Barbary pirates. Africa is the country of slavery *par excellence*.

But in one sense—in the sense that we tend to think of the slave trade today—the story ends with the arrival of that column at Mourzouk. Up to that time, when the Turks were in control of the Fezzan, the trade still existed in its traditional form. The Arab dealers were still able to round up victims in the Central African villages and smuggle their merchandise across the unpoliced caravan routes northwards to the south Mediterranean ports for trans-shipment to the Middle Eastern sultanates where there was (and still is) a regular demand for eunuchs, catamites, and young girls.

A few of the old men who squat outside the bazaars on the main street of Mourzouk remember the caravans arriving from the Chad and Niger River territories; their sons, on the other hand, know nothing about this aspect of the slave trade. There is very little left to remind them of it. Columns of Negroes yoked together coming up out of the desert under the whips of their slave masters are as much a mirage to them as to a European boy. The Turkish fort where the commander exacted a poll tax from the traders and helped himself to the more interesting merchandise is to these Libyan boys another abandoned ruin in which they play hopscotch or chase scorpions. The old slave compound where the Negroes were rested before the next stage of their march is now a public square where vegetables, fruit, goats, and scraggy chickens are sold on market days.

So the traveller who expects to find sensational reminders of the slave trade will be disappointed. The Arab *razzias* or raids on Negro villages, the long columns of wretched men, women, and children marching across the desert, the herding of victims into slave ships, all belong to history. Officially, slavery had been abolished throughout Africa.

Yet it survives and persists; and is, in fact, endemic to the continent. And there are many reasons why this is so—the most obvious of which is the economic one. Where there are no machines to do the work needed for even basic survival some form of human servitude is inevitable. The whole world up to the Industrial Revolution was built and run on this principle. The principle still obtains in non-industrial Africa.

For this reason among others, the Treaty for the Repression of African Slave Trade signed by the world powers at Brussels in 1890, the League of Nations which tackled the problem at a Special Slavery Convention in 1926, and the United Nations which have been investigating the question since 1951 have had little success in suppressing what are actually age-old institutions and practices.

'Slavery', says the Rapporteur appointed by the U.N., 'appears to be a social institution. It is in harmony with the system of social, economic, religious, and political values of the peoples that practise it.'

The most obvious of these 'values', as we have said, is the economic one. For since the principle of collective bargaining is unknown in primitive Africa, an unskilled man sells not so much his labour as himself. And if he is completely impoverished and hopelessly in debt he often has no alternative except to condemn himself to a life of bondage.

Penniless or debt-ridden Negroes of the Niger River territories, for instance, are paid a lump sum in advance to work in the ill-famed salt-mines of Taodeni in Mauretania, 360 miles north of Timbuktu. These mines are vital to the economy of the Niger and Upper Volta regions, for this part of Africa is chronically deficient in salt. In fact, so precious was this article in the old days that it was actually used as currency in Timbuktu, or bartered at the rate of a pound of salt to an ounce of gold. Because of this demand the Taodeni mines have been exploited since 1585, and some idea of their commercial value is seen from the fact that twice a year, in March and November, caravans of up to 30,000 camels form up at Timbuktu and cross the 360 miles of one of the most arid stretches of the Sahara in order to transport the rock salt of Taodeni.

Taodeni itself is probably the nearest thing to hell on earth on this planet, for the thermometer touches 127 degrees in midsummer, and there is nothing there but sand, from which the rock salt has to be dug out by miners standing knee-deep in brackish water. In the old days of the Arab and Moroccan control of the region the Negroes who worked the mines were outright slaves. Their life expectancy under these conditions was from three to five years. They were regularly replaced by men captured in the *razzias* on defenceless villages. There was nobody to question the system and nobody to protest, for no European had ever visited Taodeni until the French occupation of Mauretania at the end of the nineteenth century.

This type of debt-bondage is found wherever there are salt, gold, diamond, or coal mines in Africa. Moreover, the status of the bondsmen is worse since the colonial powers have been forced to withdraw and to leave the administration of the new states to native politicians. During the European occupation slaves could, theoretically, be freed merely by drawing the attention of the authorities to their condition, though in practice there were so many forms and degrees of servitude that no colonial administration, however well meaning, could possibly control the entire system. It is doubtful whether serfs and bondsmen have any more hope of liberation under the new régimes.

For neither the Moslem nor the pagan African has the same abhorrence of slavery as the modern Christian. To the former, Koranic law justifies slavery under certain conditions, since the Prophet, in company with his Christian contemporaries, condoned the institution as a necessary basis of society. Mohammed and his apologists laid down specific rules for the treatment of slaves: they were to be humanely treated and liberated on their conversion to Islam. There were, incidentally, no such provisos in Christian law. However, the Moslem's obligation to emancipate a converted slave was seldom respected in the case of Negroes, though usually it was respected in the case of Christian captives who renounced their faith in favour of Islam.

To-day, those states which openly condone slavery have regularised the practice by government decrees. Article Two, Part II, of King Ibn Saud's *Instructions Concerning Slaves* laid it down that:

> The slave shall have the following rights as against his owner or possessor:
> (1) the right to be fed, clothed, and housed;
> (2) the right to be well-treated and to be employed with kindness and consideration and without harshness;
> (3) the right to free medical attention.

Again, Article Twelve requires slave dealers to have a government licence, and Article Thirteen appoints an official 'Inspector of Slave Affairs'. As a result of these decrees, public slave markets have been discontinued, though private dealers continue to keep a limited 'stock'—notably of boys from Ethiopia and girls from Syria.

No African country, however, whether Moslem or pagan, 'advertises' its recognition of the old practices in such forthright terms as King Ibn Saud used in his *Instructions*. They prefer to ignore or deny the existence of the institution. Yet domestic or chattel slavery still survives in the classic tradition, or in the form of the sale of children who grow up deprived of their civic rights and personal freedom. One sees these infants in the small towns and villages, sent out to do the marketing when they are not engaged in household chores. This sweated child labour is often given a quasi-legal form under the guise of 'adoption'. We would call it outright slavery; and the impression is that it will take more than U.N. Commissions to eradicate it.

The European colonial administrators and the Christian missionaries fought against such practices with only superficial success, one obvious reason being the difficulty of interfering in what were actually family affairs. Thus, in many parts of Africa, the trade in children has the apparent sanction of

Moslem or tribal custom. The agent who comes to a village to buy children has only to represent himself as a marriage-broker and to bring presents to the chief to be welcome. Young girls are produced, usually from seven to nine years of age, who are sold by their parents on the grounds of poverty. Even if the authorities tried to punish such offences under the European code they would have difficulty in finding witnesses prepared to testify against their own people.

Moreover, as regards the slaves themselves, these bonded servants know no other way of life and would be incapable of surviving alone in a patriarchial society. The descendants of slaves, too, are likely to be content with their lot, especially if they are integrated members of their master's family and are well treated. And, 'speaking very generally', says a U.N. Report, 'slaves are well treated by their masters and are regarded as forming part of a family'.

In other words, a form of domestic serfdom has replaced outright slavery all over Africa, and the reason is that the work of cultivating enough food in the oases, formerly the function of Negro slaves, has to go on. Someone has to draw up the water from the wells—a bucketful at a time, from sunrise to sunset, summer and winter. Someone has to work the little gardens which grow just enough vegetables and grain to supplement the staple diet of dates. Someone, too, has to watch the flocks of goats which roam about the desert.

These tasks almost invariably fall to the women and children, who, since they receive no set wages, have no restricted hours of work, and are given no social or political rights, belong to the category of bond-slaves or serfs.

The basis of the system is simple. The older and richer men who own land need a donkey and three or four field hands to work the well and cultivate the garden. Donkeys are cheap enough, and women cost nothing in wages if you marry them. A Moslem is legally allowed four wives, and two or three of these are likely to be young girls who are put to work on the land. Worker-wives are easily obtained under a system where daughters can be 'sold' by their parents in a contractual arrangement which is the basis of the Moslem marriage law.

Once married, a woman may be used, to all intents and purposes, as a domestic slave. She may be put to work with the donkey hauling up water from the well in a goatskin bag, or hoeing the garden, or minding the flock.

Such a patriarchial system cannot be termed outright slavery. But when it is seen that women in strictly orthodox Moslem communities are not even permitted to go shopping, or buy their own clothes, or take their sick baby to the clinic—let alone take part in civic activities—a European woman would hardly consider it to be anything else.

The bondage of both men and women in Africa, however, is bound eventually to be modified by the impact of Western ideas and methods. One sees signs of change in even the remotest oases where schools have been set up and a few little girls appear in the classrooms. It is a step towards the education and emancipation of women—a trend, incidentally, which comes from Egypt; and it is the 'liberation' of women by President Nasser that constitutes his strongest appeal to the new generation in those Moslem countries where the veil is the symbol of the old order.

In another way the discovery of oil throughout the Sahara has affected the life and thinking of nomads like the Tuareg, the 'blue-veiled men' whose social system has been based on technical slavery for centuries. The Tuareg nobles, who scorn to soil their hands by manual labour, still own slaves by custom and tradition. These slaves do all the work for their masters and belong to them psychologically as well as physically, since they are members of the tribe and are entitled to be fed, clothed, and protected. But the Tuareg are no longer the lords of the desert, and many of the poorer younger men are employed by the oil companies as truck-drivers, technicians, and ditch-diggers. They earn a weekly wage and buy their supplies in stores, like any town-dweller. The new generation has no need of slaves whom they must feed and protect. In other words, the system is becoming obsolescent.

So the continuous flow of Western ideas and attitudes into Africa, together with the introduction of modern methods and machines, may, in some indefinite future, eliminate these remnants of slavery in its many and various manifestations. Just as those scenes typical of the seventeenth century, when 300,000 Negroes were exported to Jamaica alone after being packed like sardines into the stinking holds of slave ships, will never be seen again, so examples of blatant serfdom are becoming increasingly rare.

15 *The Treatment of Slaves*

In order to understand the nature of the slave trade one must return to that lost African world which can best be glimpsed through the eyes of the first explorers. It will then be seen that whereas the commerce cannot be in any sense justified, it can at least be explained, because, in the beginning, it was Africans who sold each other to the slavers. The natives committed even greater crimes against each other than this—such barbarisms, in fact, that slavery in the European colonies was a merciful fate compared with the treatment a captive could expect from his African co-nationals. To the tribal kings in their continuous wars against each other prisoners were merely an embarrassment, to be disposed of in the quickest and most brutal manner conceivable. The German explorer Dr. Eduard Vogel, who visited Central Africa just over a hundred years ago, gives this description of the method used:

> That evening I heard a strange sound. Coming out of my tent, I saw to my horror that each of the thirty-six prisoners had been mutilated with the aid of a blunt knife: each had lost his left leg below the knee and his right arm from the elbow down. The victims lay bleeding to death on the ground. Only three of the thirty-six had been spared by the executioners—only to have their right hand chopped off, to be thus sent back to their own country to let their people see what awaited them. Useless cruelty, for two of these three also died along with the others. . . .[1]

1. Eduard Vogel, *Reisen in Central Afrika* (1859) pp. 38 ff.

In addition, many of the prisoners whose legs and arms were not chopped off were spared in order to be burnt alive as human sacrifices to the local god: it is recorded that at the death of an Ashanti queen in 1816 more than 3,500 slaves were murdered in her honour. Others—the healthiest of the young males—were castrated and kept as eunuchs. The mortality rate in this operation is understandable if we consider a report made by a French doctor at the beginning of this century.[1]

> Upon the order of the king, the prisoner designated for castration is seized and a cord with a slip knot is placed round his neck and tied to his right hand, thus preventing any resistance at the cost of strangling himself. The victim is laid on the ground where six strong young men hold him down in such a way that the operative area is level with a fairly large hole that has been previously dug in the ground. His head is covered with a sack. After having shaved the area, the operator puts a tight lashing round both the penis and testicles at the root of the penis. Taking his curved, two-edged knife and holding the genitals in his left hand, he cuts round slowly, beginning underneath and so up to the pubic hairs, making a veritable circular incision. He then proceeds with an actual excision of the organ. No attempt is made to stop the bleeding; they wait for the haemorrhage to stop of itself. For want of anything better, they turn the patient over on to his front so that the open wound is over the hole, while one of the attendants bends the right foot up towards the victim's back in order to increase the flow of blood.
>
> The patient who has lost consciousness and who has the good luck to survive (for the mortality rate, as one would expect, is extremely high) is propped up in a standing position until the haemorrhage stops, then made to drink. After that, he is laid down again and left for two or three days while the wound is spread over with a salve made of butter. The unhappy man remains like this, lying in the hut, without any surgical dressing, shaken by incessant vomitings and subject to the most atrocious sufferings, particularly in the region of the bladder—micturition having become a torture. He is unable to take the least nourishment.

1. Dr. E. Ruelle, 'Notes anthropologiques sur quelques populations noires de l'Afrique Occidentale Française', *L'Anthropologie*, 1904, pp. 680 ff.

At the end of this period, they proceed to bathe the wound with a concoction made from two special trees—the *Noera* and the *mougoudero*. If the patient is in very great pain, they bathe the wound four times a day, once during the night. Generally the sick man is only able to get up after the seventeenth day when he is able to get as far as the door of his hut. But he doesn't fully recover for at least a month and a half. When he is back on his feet, he is sent to the king who puts him in charge of the prisoners of war and the harem.

We succeeded in examining one of these eunuchs, or rather, the chief eunuch. He was a man of 35 to 40, tall, strong, and well made. He had been subjected as a prisoner to this atrocious mutilation at the age of 15. The operation, he said, was done very slowly and the pain was such that he lost consciousness. He had no memory of what was done for him afterwards. When he regained consciousness, he found himself mutilated and the wound covered with a white powder.

On examination, I saw not a trace of the genital organs: penis, scrotum—everything was excised right up to the abdomen. Among the pubic hair, though sparse, there could be discerned a sort of vagina formed in the middle part of the excision, with thick lateral folds—giving the impression of very thick lips. The external orifice of the urethra was concealed within these folds.

The eunuch was plump, but not obese. His voice was normal. When asked if there had been any change in his manner of speaking after the castration, he told us he had never noticed any. He had developed normally.

All the journals of the early African travellers report, without exception, similar cases of barbarism not only towards prisoners-of-war but towards the members of their own tribe and families. Cruelty, as one explorer states, seemed to be the 'national sport'. René Caillié, the first European to reach Timbuktu and to return to tell the tale, gives a hundred instances of this insatiable desire to inflict pain for the pleasure of watching another person suffer.

My sufferings were a diversion. If they found me lying almost senseless on the ground, expiring with thirst, they pulled my clothes and pinched me, finishing always by asking me to drink some brandy and eat some pork, and then bursting into roars of laughter.[1]

Under these conditions and among a people who had no concept whatsoever of the dignity, let alone the sanctity, of human life, prisoners-of-war, outcasts, and those without property or rights were lucky to survive at all, even as slaves. The alternative, as we have seen, was to be killed like unwanted animals. And until the Arabs organised the disposal of captives by barter the system of massacring prisoners was standard practice. Once the value of human life was demonstrated in the form of gifts or cash, however, the native chieftains were eager to co-operate in the trade to such an extent that if the numbers were inadequate, they had no scruples about including members of their own families in the consignment. When the demand for black labour could no longer be met by the African kings themselves, the Arabs organised their own *razzias*, while the European merchants operating from the forts along the coasts supplied native hunting parties with guns and powder and, at the sound of a horn, these posses set off into the interior, to return a few months later with their 'bag'.

The captives were marched to the coast in long columns, usually chained together by neck shackles. They were kept moving by the whip, the slave-master's sign of office. On reaching the port of embarkation, they were put in cells or pens to await a slave ship bound for the Americas. While in these assembly stations they were examined by the ships' captains and surgeons, since the old and sick were obviously not likely to survive the Middle Passage, as the crossing to the West Indies was called. Those selected for shipment were branded on the chest with the owner's initial or trademark. 'We take all possible care', a Dutch slave dealer wrote, 'that they are not burnt too much, especially the women who are more tender than the men.'[2]

1. René Caillié, *Travels through Central Africa*, 1839, pp. 126–7.
2. W. Bosman, *A New and Accurate Description of the Coast of Guinea*, 1705, p. 23.

The danger now was the possibility of an insurrection, though the docility of the Negroes made this unlikely. Probably they considered themselves lucky not to have been murdered outright. But, as a precaution, men and women alike were stripped naked, packed into the slave ship, and riveted to the floor by a long chain passed through their ankle shackle. The crew's job was to stow aboard as many slaves as was physically possible according to specific measurements. A full-grown male was allowed 6 ft. × 1 ft. 4 in. of space; a full-grown female 5 ft. 10 in. × 1 ft. 4 in.; a boy, 5 ft. × 1 ft. 2 in.; and a girl 4 ft. 6 in. × 1 ft. The result of these stowage calculations is illustrated in the plan of the British slaver *Brookes*, a barque of 320 tons permitted by law to carry 454 slaves.[1]

The danger of revolt from over 400 fear-crazed men, even though shackled, was countered by turning the quarter-deck and forecastle into miniature forts in which two members of the crew kept continuous watch with their guns at the ready. At the slightest suggestion of revolt every white man on board opened fire into the holds where the slaves lay on the floor.

The conditions on board a slaver, what with the overcrowding, heat, dysentery, and animal fear of savages who had never seen the sea and were sometimes convinced that they were being sold for white men's meat, are summed up in one captain's evidence before the Lords of the Committee of Council appointed in 1789 to inquire into the slave trade and plantations.

> We made the most of the room and wedged them in. They had not so much room as a man in his coffin either in length or breadth. It was impossible for them to turn or to shift with any degree of ease . . . When in rough weather the scuttles were closed, the slaves drew their breath with all those laborious and anxious efforts for life which are observed in expiring animals, subjected by experiment to foul air, or in the exhausted receiver of an air pump.[2]

As with all vital statistics connected with the trade, the

1. Thomas Clarkson, *The Cries of Africa to the Inhabitants of Europe*, (1821), p. 26.
2. *Report Before the Lords*, 1789, pp. 34, 35.

number and proportion of slaves who died in the course of the Middle Passage cannot be calculated, since the mortality rate varied with the conditions. In a very bad storm at sea, cargo, crew, and the ship herself would be lost. In cases where slaves were packed in on top of their rations of yams, rice, and horse-beans, one case of dysentery would spread within a couple of days or so to the entire contingent. Then, indeed, the holds of the slaver became a stinking, groaning hell, with as many as two out of three dying. They died not only from dysentery and suffocation, but from self-inflicted wounds, or by leaping overboard in mid-ocean, or by starving themselves. Captains of the slave ships admitted in Parliament that they expected to lose one out of four slaves on a bad crossing and that the best they could hope for under favourable conditions was to deliver alive only 90 per cent of their human cargo. Desperate cases, on the other hand, required desperate remedies. When an English slave ship with 400 slaves aboard went aground off Jamaica, the crew took to the boats and landed safely on a small island with their arms and provisions. Here they passed the night. Next morning they discovered that their ship had not broken up and that the men slaves had extricated themselves from their irons and had made rafts on which they were ferrying some women and children to the shore by swimming alongside. As this small armada approached, the crew opened fire and killed over 300 of them, then returned to their vessel, overpowered the remainder of the Africans, and, warping the ship off the rocks, proceeded to Kingston where the remaining thirty-four slaves were sold. In the court of judicature at the Guildhall the loss of the other slaves was adjudged to fall on the owners of the vessel and not the underwriters. The question of murder did not arise.

The treatment of the survivors when they reached the American colonies, either in the West Indies, where they were sold to the sugar planters, or in the southern states of America, where they were to work in the cotton fields, is the last and most inhuman chapter in the history of the slave trade. Two characteristic laws illustrate the attitude of the white masters and the status of the black slaves: one, enacted by the legislature of Barbados in 1717, stated that a slave who ran away and was absent for thirty days should have his feet cut off; a second, passed in the West Indies in 1783, upheld the principle 'that it was in any master's power to torture or even murder his slave with impunity, and this in the sight of a thousand black spectators, provided he only took care that no white person beheld him'.

In actual practice, cutting off a slave's feet, mutilating, or murdering him was rarely necessary. Discipline was enforced by the cowhide whip. In well-organised communities there was a professional whipper called a 'jumper', who went the rounds scourging delinquent slaves, and it was the expert's boast that every one of his lashes 'brought flesh'. One colonial housewife stipulated that the slaves should be flogged every Monday morning on the grounds that it was good for them. In the absence of a professional 'jumper', friends, neighbours, or hirelings were always ready to whip Negroes as a disciplinary precaution.

Plantation life was not all flagellation, of course. If a slave worked well and never fell foul of his overseer he could survive. The Reverend James Ramsay, who administered to the spiritual welfare of the West Indian plantation owners in the 1780s, gives a detailed account of a day in the life of a sugar slave.[1]

4 a.m.:	The plantation bell rings. Slaves go to the fields.
9.00–9.30:	Breakfast eaten in the field.
Noon:	Collecting blades and tufts of grass for the master's horses and cattle.
2.00:	Assembly. Slaves who return with an inadequate bundle of grass get 4–10 lashes with the whip. Dinner.
3.00–7.00:	Strong slaves work in the plantation; old and weak slaves 'culling grass blade by blade'.
7.00–8.00:	Supper.
8.00–midnight:	During the harvest strong slaves and animals required for boiling the sugar cane.
Sundays:	Slaves allowed to work their own vegetable 'patch'.

1. *An Essay on the Treatment and Conversion of African Slaves in the British Sugar Colonies*, 1784.

The Reverend Ramsay considered that this fifteen- to twenty-hour day was too long, and he objected to many other aspects of the system. Too often the overseer was either 'a dissipated, careless, unfeeling young man, or a grovelling, lascivious, old bachelor—each with his half-score of black or mulatto harlots who, at their will, select for him among the slaves the objects of his favour or hatred'. He objects, too, to the conditions in which pregnant women had to live and recommends that 'two rooms be added to the hospital, one for the reception of the lying-in women, one for the sucking children'. Mr. Ramsay also complains of the censure heaped on him when he tried to convert slaves to a 'decent Christian way of life'. The masters accused him of interrupting work; and the slaves often would have nothing to do with the white man's religion. Typical was a group whom a local parson baptised ten at a time by rattling through the Office of Baptism as fast as he could and then throwing water into their faces. 'The slaves resented this procedure,' says Ramsay, 'for they could not remember their new name and regarded the throwing of water into their face as an affront.'

It all seemed rather hopeless to a humane Christian, and Mr. Ramsay can only conclude: 'Masters and slaves are natural enemies to each other.' However, he did not leave the matter there, but returned to England to join forces with Thomas Clarkson and William Wilberforce in their crusade to abolish the slave trade.

Throughout the eighteenth century the European merchants, working with the African chieftains, had a virtual monopoly of the trade from the River Gambia in the north to the Congo in the south. Captives taken out of these territories were marched overland to Atlantic ports like Freetown for shipment to the New World—an arrangement which left Central and Eastern Africa to the Arab traders who were supplying

Moslem countries. The Arabs used the trans-Saharan caravan routes which had been their sphere of influence since the ninth century. To speculate whether the sea or desert route was preferable from the slaves' point of view would be meaningless. The Atlantic crossing was some 2,000 miles and took anything from six weeks to three months; the journey across the Great Desert was 800 miles and was performed in sixty days. The chances of surviving by the former route appear to have been three in four; by the latter, four in five.

We have a number of eyewitness accounts of caravans crossing the desert, for many Saharan travellers from Frederick Hornemann, the first of them, made part of their journey in company with slaves. Hornemann crossed from Cairo to Mourzouk in 1798, to be followed by explorers who drew the world's attention to the horrors of the desert traffic. Typical of them was James Richardson, whose life was dedicated to exposing the trade which had, by this time, been outlawed by all European nations, but continued unabated in the Moslem world. Born in 1806 and educated for the Church, Richardson was a vehement and active abolitionist who sacrificed his life for his beliefs, for he finally died of the 'fever' in an African village. He was then forty-five, but he had by the once widely read accounts of his travels revealed, without sensationalism, the true facts of the trans-Saharan slave caravans. We find these entries in his diary for 1846.[1]

> *11th January*—This morning I visited Haj Ibrahim early, and seeing a young female very ill I remarked: 'You had better leave her with the daughter of the marabout.' He replied, much agitated, 'Oh no, it's a she-devil.' A few minutes after I heard the noise of the whipping, and turning round, I saw the Haj beating her, not very mercifully . . . (Almost immediately afterwards the girl died. The slave-merchant's servant explains:) 'Her stomach is swollen. We couldn't cure her. She had diarrhoea.' This requires no comment. The child was of some eleven years of age, and of the frailest form. Omer, before he put her in the shallow grave, felt her breast to see if she were really dead. At first he seemed to doubt it and fancied he felt her heart beating, but at last he made

1. James Richardson, *Travels in the Great Desert*, 1848, *passim*.

up his mind that she was really dead, but took some earth and stopped up her nostrils to prevent her reviving should she not be really dead. . . .

6th March—This morning Haj Essnousee, being on foot, called out for his camel to stop . . . I then saw him bringing up a slave girl about a dozen years of age, pulling her violently along. When he got her up to the camel, he took a small cord and began tying it round her neck. Afterwards he tied it round the wrist of her right arm. This done Essnousee drove the camel on . . . The wretched girl was then dragged on the ground over the sharp stones, but she never cried or uttered a word of complaint. Her legs now becoming lacerated and bleeding profusely she was lifted up by Essnousee's Arab. Thus she was dragged, limping and tumbling down, and crippled all the day, which was a very long day's journey . . . Whether she feigned sickness, or sulked, or was exhausted, I leave the reader to judge . . . Such is the power of sullen insensibility which slaves can command that brutal masters may flog them to death without finding out whether they are really ill, or only sulky. . . .

7th March—The girl dragged along yesterday had her faithful companion bringing her water and dates . . . The young women sing and sometimes dance on the road, while the boys ape the Turkish soldiers, walking in file, holding up sticks on their shoulders, and crying out 'Shoulder arms!' or words to that effect.

9th March—This forenoon a slave-girl was sadly goaded along. An Arab boy of about the same age was her tormentor who was whipping her and goading her along with a sharp piece of wood. Sometimes the young person would poke up her person. I could not see this without interfering, although I am afraid to interfere. She had got far behind, and the boy was tormenting her like a young imp. I made him take one hand, and I the other. But we could not get her up to a camel on which she might lay hold by means of a rope and so get dragged along. We then set her upon a donkey, but she was too unwell to ride, and fell off several times, the cruel rogue of a boy beating her every time she fell. What annoyed me more, her companions in bondage, those hearty and well, set-up a loud yell of laughter every time she fell off . . . I often wondered how this boy, who was some thirteen years of age, could torment these poor girls with such brutality. If he found one lagging behind, he would strip her, throw her down, and begin tormenting her in the way I have mentioned. . . .

16th March—I turned to look at one of the female slaves who was last of all, and being driven along by the whip, with several others, and thought I saw symptoms of insanity in her face. 'Why,' I observed to the driver, 'this woman is mad!' 'Mad!' he replied; 'No. She went blind yesterday.' On examining her, I found she was both blind and mad.

30th March—This evening the Negresses played their usual sweet innocent little game. They form an alley by taking hands, blocked up at the end. At the top enters one of their number backwards. As she passes along the opposite pairs, each couple put their hands across and form a seat for her by which she is bumped backwards from one seat to another seat of hands, through the whole alley . . . The point of tact is, their always sitting down on the hands, and not falling back on the ground when they would look very foolish. But as the Devil leaped over the fold of Paradise, so he may be expected to creep in everywhere, and the Negro lads are always peeping about, at a respectful distance, to see what they can see, when these falls take place; and I imagine the zest of the thing, both amongst the lads and the lassies, turns upon this naughty circumstance.

18th April—Just as we arrive at Tajourah, a Negress of tender age falls down from exhaustion, bleeding copiously from the mouth. The Arabs on foot cannot get her along. Essnousee, seeing this, called out 'Beat her! Beat her!' But the people not obeying his orders, he immediately jumped off the camel, taking with him a thick stick to beat her . . . I instantly also jumped off my camel, taking with me a stick, a match for his, calling out, 'Now, stop, stop your stick, we are now in Tripoli. No more whipping on the road . . .' I was just in the humour to give this miscreant slave dealer a thrashing.

With this incident I bid an eternal farewell to this slave caravan and now state succinctly the results of my observations on the traffic in slaves as carried on in The Great Desert of Sahara:—

1st —The slave traffic is on the increase in The Great Desert.

2nd—Many slaves are flogged to death *en route* from Ghat to Tripoli, and others are over-driven or starved to death.

3rd—The female slaves are subjected to the most obscene insults and torments by the Arab and Moorish slave-drivers; whilst the youngest females (children of four or five years of age) are violated by their brutal masters, the Tibboos, in coming from Bournou to Ghat, or Fezzan.

4th—Slave children, of five years of age, walk more than one hundred and thirty days over The Great Desert, and other districts of Africa, before they can reach the slave markets of Tripoli to be sold.

5th—Three-fourths of the slave-traffic of The Great Desert and Central Africa are supported by the money and goods of European merchants, resident in Tunis, Tripoli, Algiers, and Egypt.

Many of these incidents of the caravan trail as described by Richardson are reiterated in one form or another by all Saharan travellers as late as the beginning of this century, when the British consul Hanns Vischer was crossing the desert from Tripoli to Lake Chad, via Mourzouk.[1] All observers, with reason, were amazed at the good humour and even gaiety of the captives, who sustained each other, shared their pittance of food with the nursing mothers and babies, and when they stopped for a rest, sang, danced, and made necklaces of flowers. One can only conclude that they accepted their fate as the best they could hope for in a world which, from their experience, knew neither justice nor mercy.

1. Hanns Vischer, *Across the Sahara*, 1910.

16 *European Slaves in Africa*

The enslavement of Africans was universally accepted as a legitimate commercial enterprise until the beginning of the nineteenth century during which period the slave trade was outlawed by Christian nations, beginning with Denmark in 1803 and ending with Brazil in 1888. It had taken 400 years for the civilised world to admit that the buying and selling of Negroes was morally wrong. It should not, however, surprise us that this change of heart took so long, since slavery in some form or the other had been the economic basis of every society since the dawn of time. Tribal kingdoms, ancient civilisations, and, indeed, pre-industrial European monarchies had all depended on cheap and expendable labour. In other words, the necessity of slave labour in unmechanised societies had always been a fact of life; and the justification of the system has been logically argued by an African in this manner.

> Slavery, you say, is bad. I agree that it is bad, but slave labour is to the interior of Africa what steam power is in Europe. In your great factories where steam is used, is all well with the employés? Is there not much misery and suffering? You admit there is. Well, if the Angel of God came and saw the unhappiness of your factories and said, 'This must not continue—abolish steam', would you think it a wise decree?[1]

In contrast to the white man's endorsement of the Negro slave trade was his indignation at the bondage imposed on members of his own race by Africans, an activity which was

1. A conversation with Zebehr Pasha in 1920, reported by Sir F. D. Lugard in *The Dual Mandate*, 1923.

always condemned as a most heinous crime. Yet notwithstanding the protests of governments and churches, the European nations took no concerted action to stamp out the white slave trade but, to the contrary, tacitly condoned the practice as an inevitable consequence of their continuous wars and rivalries. It is true that the more powerful states periodically attempted by unilateral measures to restrict the excesses of the Barbary pirates who were the entrepreneurs in the white slave trade. These measures consisted of occasional naval bombardments of the pirates' lairs along the Atlantic and Mediterranean coasts, though the usual recourse was the payment of ransom money, sometimes by the Church, sometimes by private organisations, and sometimes by the families of the captives.

But despite the warlike posturing of the Christian states in the face of this insult to their sovereignty, European and American captives arrived by the shipload for almost six centuries at the African ports of Salé, Tangier, Algiers, Tunis, and Tripoli, to be sold as chattels in the busy slave markets. In addition, almost every sailor who was wrecked along the North African coasts was pounced upon by the natives and treated not as a prisoner, but as a slave. A few who survived and actually returned to their homeland gave an account of their ordeal; but, in general, their enslavement ended with their death. Precise figures of the numbers of white slaves in Africa are not available, though we do have some evidence of the total from contemporary records. There is, for instance, the claim of two organisations founded by the Catholic Church for the express purpose of ransoming Christians enslaved by the infidel. The Trinitarians (founded 1198) and the Mercedarians (1218) state that they liberated upwards of 2,000,000 Europeans in the 500 years of their operations. To this number (which cautious students might be inclined to question) must be added several thousands ransomed by Protestant missions, government agencies, and private individuals.

The fact that Christians in such numbers were bought and sold by Africans tends to have been overlooked in our preoccupation with the slave trade that flowed in the reverse direction: that is, out of Africa into the Christian territories. Yet both forms of the inhuman traffic had profound effects on the course of political history, some of which are still being felt today. Certainly one result of Barbary piracy and the enslavement of white captives by the North African states was the justification put forward by the French in 1830 to invade Algeria and so to embark on their vast African colonial conquests, 'for the benefit of Christendom', as their statesmen announced. In one sense, the French were right: the white slave trade terminated almost overnight. The Barbary pirates were swept from the seas; the slave markets where the Christians were paraded were shut down; and the *bagnios*, or underground prisons, where they were incarcerated for the night were filled in.

Indeed, so slight is the evidence of white slavery today that few tourists visiting North Africa have any inkling that tens of thousands of their forefathers walked the streets of almost every city as the bond servants of Berbers and Moors. Even a name like Salé, once as familiar to every citizen of the Western world as Timbuktu, awakens no echoes of the past, though to visit this Moroccan port is to catch a glimpse of another lost African world, within full view of the modernised city of Rabat, capital of Morocco and the site of an international airport.

Salé is worth visiting, for, like the oasis Mourzouk in Libya, it has survived almost unchanged from the heyday of slavery. Aloof and mysterious, it is still shut in behind massive towers and high ramparts. One crosses to it from Rabat by ferry and lands on the beach under the city walls. Out ahead lies the Atlantic, its huge rollers breaking over the reefs. On either side stretch the golden sands, deserted except for an occasional fisherman. And behind stand the ramparts of the most infamous pirate-lair of history—the home of the 'Salee Rovers'.

It was from this Moroccan town that the best-known character in British fiction began the odyssey we know as *The Strange, Surprising Adventures of Robinson Crusoe*. For before he was cast away on his desert island Crusoe was a slave for two years in Salé.

> Our ship [writes Defoe] making her course towards the Canary Islands, or rather between those islands and the African shore, was surprised, in the grey of the morning, by a Moorish rover. . . . We were obliged to yield and were all carried prisoners into Salee, a port belonging to Morocco.

One needs a vivid imagination to visualise Salé as it was in the time of Robinson Crusoe, for there is little left to remind the traveller of this once-powerful maritime republic to whom the European monarchs sent ambassadors to negotiate the liberation of the white slaves. The emissaries of Charles I, in fact, had to negotiate from a position of considerable weakness, since during that monarch's reign the Sallateens virtually blockaded the southern coasts of England and Ireland and periodically landed to take off the entire population of villages. On the night of June 20th, 1631, for instance, the corsairs landed at Baltimore near Cork and abducted every man, woman, and child in the hamlet—237 people in all, including William Gunter, his wife, and seven sons. Five years later they raided the South Coast of England, abducted men, women, and children, and with the permission of the French marched their captives overland to Marseilles for shipment to Algiers. Again, in 1640, not content with taking off sixty men, women, and children from St. Michael's Mount in Cornwall, they blockaded the West Coast and the British Channel so that British sailors and fishermen refused to go to sea. Shortly afterwards, as a result of a treaty between the British Crown and the beylical states, the latter were actually granted the right to halt and search British vessels on the high seas. However, the English could hardly complain, for it was British renegades who taught the non-seafaring Moors the art of piracy, and we hear of two of them who 'lived like bashaws' as a result of their crimes.

But what does remain of Salé is architecturally imposing and there are few more interesting fortified cities on the Atlantic than this pirates' stronghold. The ramparts, forty feet high and six feet thick, were built by Spanish slaves brought out of the peninsula after the Arab conquest. They continue to encircle the city with their eight gates through one of which Robinson Crusoe entered to begin his two-year term of slavery. Inside the castellated walls the modern population appears to live without any recollection of the past. The ramparts themselves are neglected except for the boys who play around the rusty cannon which once pointed out to sea to reply to the British or French navies which periodically bombarded the city—without noticeable effect. On the famous beach, a few ragged natives wander about in search of cockles. Beyond the Atlantic rollers a reef has formed, so that boats can no longer cross the bar; and the canal by which the corsairs' barques once entered the city is now filled in with rubble. Its past forgotten, and without any particular function in the future, Salé remains a monument of still another lost world of Africa.

That world—the realm of the sultans and beys—was, until recently, separate and distinct from Europe and Western civilisation, the two only meeting on the field of battle or in occasional diplomatic confrontations, neither of which lessened their hostility or solved their basic differences. Yet both had one thing in common: the solution of their manpower problem by the use of slaves and serfs. Each side exploited this system at the expense of the other. Thus, during the later Crusades the Christians employed Moslem captives to man their galleys, while the Moslems employed Christians for the same purpose. Jean de la Valette, Grand Master of the Knights of St. John (the capital of Malta is named after him), toiled for years at the oar of a Turkish galley. Dragut, the admiral of the Turkish fleet, did likewise in the galley of the Italian Andrea Doria. The galley slaves lived and died under conditions of indescribable horror, as this description by one of them writing in 1713 makes clear:

> Imagine six men shackled to a bench, naked as they were born, one foot on the floor, the other raised against the bench in front. The six hold an enormous oar, with those on the bench in front bending down in time so that the oar can pass over their back. When the oar had been thrust forward, the blade is thrust into

> the sea. This done, the rowers throw themselves backwards and fall back on to the bench which bends under their weight. Sometimes the galley is rowed thus for 10, 12, or even 20 hours at a time. On these occasions, the boatswain and sailors feed the oarsmen a morsel of bread dipped in wine. If a slave drops, he is whipped until he gets back to work. If he can't get up, he is thrown overboard, without ceremony . . . The odour on calm hot days is frightful. Flies rule the day; fleas and lice both day and night.[1]

It is obvious that there were no volunteers for this kind of life, so that the ships had to be manned either by slaves or by so-called criminals, like the hundreds of French Protestants sent to the galleys for life by Louis XIV. The larger galleys needed 400 men to work the fifty oars. As there were thousands of such vessels engaged in the endless Mediterranean wars and continuous piracy, the demand for rowers was enormous.

In brief, wars and piracy were the principal means of meeting that demand as well as supplying slaves of both sexes and all conditions. The Moslems, for their part, needed, in addition to strong men to man their fleets, work the mines, and erect their buildings, European specialists and skilled artisans. Neither the Arabs, Turks, nor Moors were technically advanced, and their great public monuments—palaces, castles, forts, and mosques—from Constantinople round through North Africa to Spain were largely the work of European architects and master builders. Even the pirate ships in the case of the Salee Rovers were constructed for them by British shipwrights who had turned renegade.

Once the captives were brought off the pirates' ships and driven to the slave markets in the North African ports, they were judged by their physical condition and skills. Who they were, what was their social status in their own communities, whether they were aristocrats or commoners, educated or illiterate—all these factors made no difference to the dealers or buyers. Just as African kings toiled in the sugar plantations of the Barbados, so European nobles languished in the subterranean prisons of Barbary. Murrough O'Brien, 1st Earl of Inchiquin, was a slave in Algiers for six months. The Scottish

1. Jurien de la Gravière, *Les Derniers Jours de la Marine à Rames*, 1885.

lairds of Morton and Oliphant were imprisoned in the same city for four years, which the French nobleman Le Sieur Jean Baptiste Gramaye described from personal experience as 'Hell's Epitome, Misery's Ocean, Christian Whirlpool, Torture's Centre, Hell upon Earth, Whip of the Christian World'.

It will be seen from the list of European captives who stood on the auctioneer's block in the Barbary markets that slavery, whatever else it was, was certainly a great leveller. Some of the prisoners brought ashore were in their finery, others in their rags. The former always fetched more in view of their potential ransom. Lord Inchiquin was a particularly good investment, since he was eventually released on payment of 7,500 crowns, or £75,000. Others, like Cervantes, had to wait longer. One of those whose ransom took some time to negotiate was Captain Sir Jeffrey Hudson, the self-styled officer and knight who stood 3 ft. 6 in. in his socks. (He was only 1 ft. 9 in. when he was first brought to the attention of the Duchess of Rutland by his proud parents.) However, what this mannikin lacked in height, he made up for in importance, for he was to become none other than Charles I's favourite dwarf, trusted enough to have been sent by the monarch to escort back from Paris a midwife for Queen Charlotte. On the return voyage he had been captured by Flemish pirates, but was ransomed by his royal patron.

A few years later he was not so lucky. He happened to be again in Paris on king's business when he challenged the brother of Lord Croft to a duel, for, as a contemporary says of him, 'he was a dwarf, but no dastard'. His noble opponent arrived for the encounter armed with a syringe. He was promptly shot dead by Sir Jeffrey, who preferred a horse pistol. Fleeing from Paris and crossing the Mediterranean, he was captured by Algerine pirates and sold as a slave. Unfortunately, Sir Jeffrey, though he lived to a ripe old age, didn't write an account of his eight years' servitude, and all we know about it was that he grew another 1 ft. 9 in. taller 'as a result of numerous hardships, much labour, and frequent beating'.

If this peppery little man's claim is correct he must have been one of the few Christian slaves who benefited physically from his ordeal. The accounts left by other captives tell another story—of near-starvation as well as 'frequent beating'. There are a number to choose from, including Cervantes's description of his five years' servitude in Algiers, during which time he made two attempts to escape. On the second occasion he was again caught and sentenced to be bastinadoed with 2,000 strokes; but luckily for him, and for us, the sentence was never inflicted. Cervantes was eventually ransomed by his mother in 1580.

But very few of the English captives had families who could afford the ransom money demanded by the Moors and, as we shall see, the British Government was almost indifferent to the misfortunes of the seamen and passengers taken by the Barbary pirates and sold into slavery. Only a few managed to escape and to return home, where they told their horrendous tale in books with titles like *Barbarian Cruelty! an Accurate Account of the Sufferings of British Captives*; and *A History of the Long Captivity*. The tone of these narrations, with their bits of 'fine writing', their moral reflections, and occasional Latin tags, suggests that they were the work of hacks employed to exploit the interest in shipwrecks and piracy popularised by Daniel Defoe. But there is no doubt that the facts are, for the most part, true, even such statements as 'We were now reduced to that Pitch of Distress that we began to entertain the melancholy Thought of killing one in the Company (by lot), for the Support and Maintenance of the Rest'.

The account of the eighteenth-century English sailor Thomas Pellow is certainly trustworthy, since he admitted to becoming a Moslem, which took both courage and honesty at a time when the Infidel was equated with Satan himself. Pellow tells us that he was given as a porter to one of the wives of Moulay Ismail, the bloodthirsty Sultan of Morocco, who was reputed to have had 80,000 women in his seraglio. Later on, as a slave labourer on some of the enormous palaces in Fez and Meknes built by gangs of European captives, he was an eyewitness of this monstrous monarch's cruelty.

> The Emperor's wrath is terrible which the Christians have often felt. One day, passing by a high wall on which they were at

> work, and being affronted that they did not keep time in their strokes, as he expects they should, he made his guards go up and throw them off the wall, breaking their legs and arms, knocking them on the head in a miserable manner. Another time he ordered them to bury a man alive and beat him down along with the mortar in the wall.[1]

Pellow's account of the cruelty and tortures he witnessed is confirmed by other slaves who escaped and lived to tell the tale. Christians who refused to renounce their faith had their nails wrenched off by pincers; their hands sacked up in bags of quicklime and salt; their bodies incarcerated in boxes lined with sharp spikes or stuffed into ovens in which they were slowly baked. An English merchant residing at Tetuan in Morocco writes home:

> Yesterday Mr. Noble and I were passing by the prison when we saw a man hanging by his heels, with irons upon his legs, pinchers upon his nose, his flesh cut with scissors, and two men perpetually drubbing him and demanding money. When the fellow was not able to speak, they renewed their blows; and this was a bought man that they gave 500 ducats for and expect by sheer torture to force out of him 500 ducats more.[2]

But while there is no doubt whatsoever that the sultans and beys used both their slaves (and their own subjects, for that matter) with inhuman cruelty, the overall record of the Moslem treatment of Christian captives compares favourably with the Christians' attitude towards enslaved Africans. The latter were invariably regarded and treated as subhuman, without rights and without hope of any amelioration of their lot. The Moslems, on the other hand—always with the exception of the brutal tyrants—were sometimes humane, sometimes even correct in their relations with their European slaves. Everything depended, of course, on the master. The sultans, beys, and governors always had first choice, and their requirements were for skilled labourers who built most of the palaces, bridges, and fortifications today admired by tourists

1. Thomas Pellow, *A History of the Long Captivity*, p. 63.
2. Sir R. L. Playfair, *The Scourge of Christendom* (1884), p. 121.

to Fez, Meknes, Marrakesh, and other cities of North Africa. Thousands of these European artisans were employed as brick-makers, stone-masons, carpenters, and mechanics. The second requirement was for young or comely females who were automatically sent to the harems. Many of these women and girls became the wives or concubines of sultans and the mothers of princes.

Unfortunately they left us no account of their experiences, though we occasionally hear vague rumours of them. We hear, for instance, of a Scottish girl called Mary Gray, captured by the Salee Rovers early in the reign of James I and sent to the harem of the Sultan of Morocco where she became such a favourite that she was allowed to send for her brother. This Andrew Gray made a fortune as a merchant in Morocco and eventually returned to Edinburgh where he erected a mansion in the Canongate and lived in fine style, thanks to his sister. It would seem that he had certain qualms of conscience about the manner in which he acquired his fortune, because he erected a plaque over his gate with the statue of a Moor and the legend, *Miserere mei, Domine. A peccato, debito, et morte subita Libera me.* 1.6.1618. Perhaps the *libera* also refers to his sister Mary, who, like the other European wives and concubines of the sultans, never came home again.

The historian John Windus, who accompanied a British mission sent by George I to Morocco to make a peace treaty with the Emperor Moulay Ismail and to ransom British slaves held by that monarch, actually spoke to one such woman—a 'poor unhappy Englishwoman who had been taken two years before we came to Mequinez, was forced to turn Moor, and lived in the palace. She recounted that the very excrements and spittle which came from the Emperor were preserved in little boxes by his women, as believing that anything that came from him would keep them from all distempers.'[1]

More fortunate was an Englishwoman called 'Mrs. Crisp of Minorca', who recounts her near-brush with concubinage in a curious little volume called *The Female Captive*, published in 1769. Mrs. Crisp was aboard a British ship bound from

1. John Windus, *A Journey to Mequinez*, 1725, p. 95.

Gibraltar to London when it was stopped on the high seas by the Salee Rovers. The English lady tartly remarks that she was 'tormented by the impertinent discourses of those merciless Moors', who eventually ceased talking and took her captive aboard their privateer. She admits, however, that the 'Admiral', as she calls the pirate captain, treated her courteously. Moreover, she was well housed in Salé and even entertained as a distinguished foreign guest. Introduced to the 'Apartment of the Ladies', she 'underwent a mortifying Examination from these indelicate Females', who, one would imagine, were merely interested in her clothes and appearance. She ate a little, 'in compliment to her Host, having heard they esteem it a Favour for the Christians to partake of their Repast when invited'. But apart from partaking of repasts, she made no concessions to her captors, but, to the contrary, overawed them to the extent that orders were given 'to travel gently to the Palace of the Emperor in Marrakesh, resting in the Day, and proceeding on the Night, that I might not be too much fatigued with the Heat'. She was, she tells us, in tears most of this time, though her worst ordeal was to have been bitten by bedbugs in Marrakesh. Arriving at the Moorish capital, she was treated very courteously by the Sultan, who already had one English girl as his wife, together with an assortment of French, Spanish, and Portuguese consorts. The Sultan entertained her to a banquet and 'begged her to become his Concubine, but my Tears flowed incessantly and exceedingly affected him'. The upshot was that she was sent out of the palace and allowed to go home to Mr. Crisp. Her adventures, in fact, sound like the daydreams of a Victorian lady novelist, but they are quite factual and give another aspect of the treatment of Christian captives by Moslem pirates and princes.

Mrs. Crisp was not the only Christian prisoner to have been treated so generously by her captors. No less an illustrious slave than St. Vincent de Paul (1580–1660) testifies to the humanity of his Moslem masters during his two years' servitude in Tunisia after being captured in the Mediterranean by Barbary pirates. Vincent, of course, was lucky, as his story shows, but his experience was not untypical. He was first bought in the Tunis slave market by a fisherman, which, in itself, implies how numerous and cheap Christian prisoners were at that time if a fisherman could afford to own one. The fisherman, however, hastened to get rid of him, since 'nothing is so antipathetic to me as the sea'. He was next purchased by an elderly alchemist—'an extremely humane and tolerant man', who had been working for fifty years to find the philosopher's stone.

'He loved me dearly', Vincent writes, 'and amused himself by talking to me about alchemy.' When this amiable old man died, he willed Vincent to his nephew, described as 'a veritable anthropomorphite'; and this odd personage (for it is not easy to understand what exactly Vincent means by his expression) sold his slave to a French renegade who had received as a reward for his apostasy an estate from the Bey, together with three beautiful wives—one Greek, another Turkish, and a third not identified. It was the Turkish wife who, according to Vincent, 'served as the instrument in the immense mercy of God to deliver me from my bondage'. In more prosaic terms, this lady used to visit the captive every day in the fields where he was digging ditches on the French renegade's estate. She came, it appears, in order to hear him sing his Christian hymns in praise of the Lord. For, 'she took so much pleasure in my singing that she no longer believed in the Paradise of her fathers, but felt such emotion while I was doing it that she avowed it was something marvellous'. Vincent's concerts for the Turkish wife continued for ten months, at the end of which period she helped him escape and he arrived back in good health and spirits in his native France.

It should be noted, however, that the Church authorities would just as soon omit this episode in the life of the saint, for we find an entry under Vincent's commemoration day (July 19th) in Butler's *Lives*:

> The captivity in, and romantic escape from, Tunisia raise such delicate questions and have been so controverted that, without wishing to indulge in any improper suppressions, it seems better to ignore it and to get on more solid ground.

One obvious reason for the Church's scepticism is that the adventures of Vincent de Paul were not likely to excite the horror and indignation of true Christians against the ancient enemy and rival. Indeed, the lack of these strong emotions was the very thing the Church had reason to fear, since the whole campaign of fund-raising for the ransoming of Christions was based on the public's hatred of the Infidel and fears that the slaves would renounce their faith and acknowledge Mahommed as the true prophet. To this end the organisations licensed by the Church to collect funds emphasised not the cases where slaves had been kindly treated, but those captives who had been atrociously misused and even tortured. Their chief propagandist, himself a Trinitarian, was Father Pierre Dan, whose *History of Barbary and Its Corsairs* was intended to prove 'the Infidels' cruelty, brigandage, and piracies, together with the great sufferings and cruel torments that Christian captives endure'. Father Dan's book, published in 1647, became extremely popular, and his accounts of atrocities perpetrated against Europeans determined the popular attitude towards the Moors, or Turks, as they were indiscriminately called. The Trinitarian describes how Christians were marched to the slave market 'often in chains', there to be stripped and examined like cattle before being bought. The fact that Christian slave traders were following exactly the same procedure with Africans was overlooked. More to the point as far as his readers were concerned was his report that women were bought for some potentate's seraglio where 'the sultan visits them to satisfy his shameless and false desires'. He adds that some monarchs became so enamoured of their beautiful Christian slaves that they married them and made them sultanas.

Father Dan has more sinister stories to tell than this, for he asserts that those Christians condemned to the Turkish galleys had their hands and sometimes their heads chopped off if they showed the least sign of mutinous conduct. There is no call to question the priest's veracity on this score, since such was the treatment of galley slaves in Christian as well as Moslem ships. Not many decades after Father Dan was writing about the brutality aboard Turkish galleys, Louis XIV was marching 400 Huguenot Protestants across France shackled by the neck to a long central chain and consigning them for life to the royal galleys at Toulon. For that matter, conditions on ships, whether galleys or sailing ships, have always been appalling up to within living memory.

> On some of the Yankee hell ships the things that go on are almost incredible and the captains have to be skilled surgeons to cope with the work of destruction wrought by their mates. Legs and arms broken were considered nothing; ribs stamped in by heavy sea boots had to mend as best they could; faces smashed like rotten apples by iron belaying pins had to get well or fear worse treatment; eyes closed up by a brawny mate's fist had to see. There have been many instances of men triced up in the rigging, stripped, and then literally skinned alive with deck-scrapers.[1]

But the organisations specifically engaged in ransoming Christians were not concerned so much with galley slaves as with the thousands of captives in the North African cities where, as the number of apostates showed, the Moslems were successful in undermining the faith of their victims by offering bribes in the form of land grants, wives, and position of power. In other words, it was the souls rather than the bodies of men which the Church endeavoured to save, for it must have seemed sometimes that Islam was winning the spiritual war that had been waged between Christians and Moslems since the eleventh century.

To this end the Church, through the two orders licensed for the purpose—the Trinitarians and Mercedarians—organised a crusade throughout Catholic Europe to collect funds for the ransoming of Christian slaves held by the Infidel. The crusade was mounted with all the resources available to the Church in sixteenth- and seventeenth-century France and Spain. Great processions were formed up to march through the towns and villages—a splendid spectacle of singing monks, their red and blue crosses blazed on their white tunics, followed by recently ransomed slaves brought back from Africa and dignitaries

1. Basil Lubbock, *Round the Horn Before the Mast*, 1902, p. 33.

carrying aloft crosses, banners, and holy pictures. Behind came the relatives of the freed captives, penitents, and supporters of the crusade, all weeping with joy. The rear was brought up by chanting monks and lay brothers whose function it was to collect contributions for the cause. In the evening the bells rang out, thanksgiving services were held in the churches, and there was music and dancing in the streets.

On those occasions where an expedition was about to leave for Africa a special ceremony was staged in order to ensure that the contributions were equal to the expenses of the crusade. Then, preceded by a band of trumpets, flutes, and cymbals, the monks mounted on white mules advanced two by two. One of the emissaries bound for Algiers, Tunis, Tripoli, or Constantinople carried the banner which was to be flown from the rescue ship. He was escorted by a herald who demanded of the mayors of each city visited whether there were any captives from that place to be ransomed—a symbolic request which emphasised the universality of Christian slavery. The Trinitarians were also empowered to examine the wills of the newly deceased and to claim one fifth of the estate of those who had died intestate. In the case of those who had forgotten or neglected to leave a legacy to the Trinitarian order, the monks demanded a contribution equivalent to the largest benefaction mentioned in the dead man's will.

There was, inevitably, a certain amount of resentment on the part of lay Christians to these methods of fund-raising, but the principal cause of dissension arose from the rivalry between the two orders themselves. The Order of the Most Holy Trinity, or Trinitarians, had been first in the field when they had sent out rescue teams as early as 1198. Basically a French order, the Trinitarians found themselves shortly to be challenged by a comparable Spanish society, the Mercedarians, who accompanied the national armies and fleets on their explorations and conquests, including those of Columbus to the New World. Relations between these two redemptionist orders were acrimonious from the beginning and finally became such an explosive religious and political issue that popes and kings had to intervene to keep some sort of peace, for each side had reached the point of accusing the other of being swindlers and mercenaries of their respective armies. The basic reason for the dispute was that each order claimed the monopoly of collecting alms, so that when the two teams arrived to work the same district their hostility took the form of quarrels which, on occasions, nearly brought France and Spain to the verge of open war. And matters were no better in the field, for we find that in the year 1644, when both Trinitarians and Mercedarians were simultaneously ransoming slaves in Algiers, the rival monks actually endangered each others' lives and safety. The Mercedarian Father Brugière had to be left behind as a hostage for the ransom money owed to the divan of Algiers. The Trinitarian Father Herault refused to advance the necessary sum on behalf of his brother priest. Result: the enraged Algerians, seeing one Christian priest sail away without ransoming the other, threw Father Brugière into prison, where he died two years later. By such incidents the enmity of the two societies reached such a pitch that each accused the other of every conceivable stratagem, including causing storms at sea with the intent of wrecking each others' ships.

In comparison with the Catholic Church's crusade the Protestants were far less active, and those agencies in Protestant countries which occupied themselves with this international bartering were, for the most part, lay organisations which went about the business of ransoming their countrymen in an unspectacular manner. One such organisation was the Worshipful Company of Ironmongers, one of whose members, Thomas Betton, had left the sum of £4,000 in 1785 for the redemption of British slaves. It follows that Protestant money was used to ransom Protestants, Catholic funds for Catholics, a principle which was to cause hard feelings between Christians themselves, while puzzling and irritating the rapacious Moors. The unwillingness of the two sects to co-operate for the common good is exemplified by the refusal of a Catholic mission led by Father Comelin to accept a fourth slave the Dey of Tunis had offered for nothing in return for the £3,000 the priest had agreed to pay for three French captives. Unluckily for him, the fourth man was a Lutheran.

17 *The Suppression of Piracy*

Despite the rivalry between the Trinitarians and Mercedarians, and their long internecine struggle for supremacy in the field, there is no doubt that the Catholic countries were far more concerned with the tragic fate of their enslaved nationals than the Protestant British were with theirs. It is true that a few humanitarians like Thomas Betton of the Worshipful Company of Ironmongers (he had been a slave in Morocco himself) provided funds for the ransoming of Englishmen held in subjection by the Moors, but, in general, the ransoming was left to private individuals, especially to the families of the captives. Obviously in the case of sailors and villagers snatched from their ships or their cottages by the pirates the relatives were unable to conduct the necessary negotiations, even if they could afford the ransom money. In the case of the wealthy or important the Government was able to intervene through the hard-worked consuls who acted as intermediaries. Again, on a number of occasions, the Government sent missions to the beylical states in an endeavour to ransom partly with money and partly with threats as many British slaves as they could. But, on the whole, the attitude of the Crown was one of indifference and parsimony. The abandonment of the unfortunate victims of piracy, like the condonation of piracy itself, appears to have been an unwritten rule of national policy.

The British did make one nation-wide effort to solve the problem in 1624, at which time 1,000 English captives in Algiers had been registered for release on payment of their ransom, as agreed in a treaty between the Bey of Algiers and the King of England. The question was how to finance the scheme. A start was made by requiring every member of Parliament above the rank of baron to contribute forty shillings, those below twenty shillings. In addition, every bishop and clergyman in England made an appeal for contributions during the services in cathedrals and churches. At the end of a three months' campaign the total collected was £2,848, not enough to hire and fit out a single ship for the voyage, let alone obtain the release of the captives. The result was that the enraged Bey declared that the treaty had been abrogated and threw James Frizell, the British consul, and all free British residents in his territories into prison, forcibly confiscating £6,000 of their property.

It was this same consul who several years later had to write to the Government begging that some funds be sent him, as his salary had not been paid for eight years. His petition was read at the Privy Council on March 9th, 1632, and their lordships, it is reported, showed much concern for their representative and 'were moved with compassion at the extreme affliction and miserable condition of His Majesty's subjects in captivity'—a matter which the consul had also brought to their attention. But apart from expressing their sympathy, the privy councillors took no steps to pay Mr. Frizell his overdue salary or to ransom the slaves, for we find the consul, eleven years later, again addressing the Council in what was to be his last known letter: 'I myself am brought so low, from want of means to maintain my charge, that I am likely to starve unless the Lords in their mercy should raise some unexpected succour for me . . . I doe verily believe that never any of His Majesty's Ministers hath bin soe neglected as I am.'

In brief, nothing was done during the reign of the Stuarts for their subjects in captivity, though at one stage a resolution was passed in the House of Commons that fines collected from members for coming late to prayers be distributed amongst the wives and mothers who daily attended the House petitioning the members to bring their husbands and sons home again. Whether these fines were ever imposed, or whether the sum collected amounted to more than enough to give an occasional grant to these destitute women, is not recorded.

There were a number of reasons for this *laissez-faire* attitude of British officialdom towards the enslavement of their subjects. One has already been mentioned: namely the tacit condonation of piracy by the major European powers so long as the buccaneers preyed on a rival nation's shipping. Hence no concerted action was undertaken by the Christian nations during the sixteenth, seventeenth, and eighteenth centuries to stamp out white slavery by means of an international control of the seas. True, from time to time each nation, notably the French and British, bombarded the pirate ports, but such punitive acts neither released the slaves nor changed the attitude of their masters.

Another reason for the continuance of piracy was the indifference of the ruling classes towards the welfare of the lower orders for whom little was done at home and less abroad. The merchant seamen belonged to the latter group, and since most of them had been impressed, they were tacitly regarded as felons, or, at least, expendable. In 1744 a British ship called *The Inspector* was wrecked off the coast near Tangier. The officers had their ransom arranged for them by the British consul; the crew were abandoned and eventually sold into slavery. An even worse misfortune befell the sailor Joseph Pitts of Exeter who was captured with his shipmates by an Algerine pirate in the Mediterranean, enslaved, tortured into accepting Islam, and eventually manumitted by his Moslem master after a journey to Mecca—the first Englishman to write an eyewitness account of that holy city. But on returning home to England fifteen years later he was at once impressed into the Royal Navy, in itself a form of servitude during the eighteenth century.

The third cause of the official inaction arose from the unwillingness of some consuls to get involved in the time-consuming business of negotiating the release of prisoners who arrived in the North African ports by the shiploads. These consuls were primarily commercial agents, and their own safety was uncertain enough without their getting caught up more than they had to in the internal politics of the sultanates. The nature of their occupational hazards can be judged from the reports that one English consul was bastinadoed until his feet fell off and a French consul loaded into a cannon and fired against the French fleet that was bombarding Algiers.

The consuls' difficulties in their almost impossible task of representing their governments, negotiating commercial transactions, ransoming important or rich captives, and sometimes even feeding their enslaved nationals were complicated by the fact that many white prisoners were not dissatisfied with their lot—to such an extent that a member of the British ambassador's staff in Morocco sent this report to his Government in 1727:

> I am sure that we saw captives who lived much better in Barbary than they ever did in their own country. Whatever money was sent them by their friends in Europe was their own, unless they defrauded one another, which had happened much oftener than by the Moors.

About the same time, another observer of white slavery in the Barbary States challenges the Irish priest Father de Bourk who had eloquently condemned the inhumanity of the Moors:

> Oh fie, Father! Though it is part of your function to make a dismal story of Slavery among *Infidels* (the very name of which is indeed bad enough) yet you should, methinks, adhere only to the truth. You came very lately from Marseilles where you must, or might, have seen the Turks, Moors, et cetera in much worse condition than the most unhappy beylical slave in Algiers. You likewise must needs have seen how slaves are treated in Spain, Malta, Genoa, et cetera. Thousands of Algiers captives live abundantly happier there (want of freedom excepted) than ever they can even hope to do at home; and that very many are excused with a few bastinadoes for crimes for which they would have suffered the wheel in most parts of Europe, or at least have made their exit in a halter. Therefore I say again, Father, stick to the truth![1]

1. *Several Voyages to Barbary*, by Captain Henry Boyde, 1736 (2nd edition), pp. 44–5.

There is no doubt, then, that the Moslem slave system was a mixture of extreme cruelty on the one hand and unusual solicitude on the other. The slave's fate, in other words, depended on his master. If he was unfortunate enough to be consigned to one of the gangs employed by a sultan or bey he could be expected to be treated like a felon—worked all day without remission, fed three loaves of black bread per diem, and incarcerated 500 to the dreaded *bagnios* at night, where he slept on the ground which was perpetually waterlogged. The private slave, in contrast, was, for the most part, better treated; and if the master was a civilised and humane man he was accepted as a member of the family. Again, those captives who were opportunist or cynical enough to say the magic formula, 'There is but one God and Mohammed is His prophet'—to become renegades, as the expression was—often became rich, particularly as they were allowed to run the taverns, a lucrative trade, even if a despicable one in the view of orthodox Moslems. Several well-born renegades, on the other hand, rose to positions of great trust and power, among them the French nobleman Count Joseph de Saulty who eloped with his colonel's wife, hid out in Tunis until she died, then went to Morocco, became a Moslem, and was appointed commander-in-chief to the Sultan.

But perhaps the most revealing statement by a witness of white slavery has been left us by General William Eaton, U.S. consul at Tunis, who wrote to his wife on April 6th, 1799:

> Truth and justice demand from me the confession that the Christian slaves among the barbarians of Africa are treated with more humanity than the African slaves among the professing Christians of civilised America.

Statements like these—one by an embassy official, one by a sailor, and one by a consul—throw a different light on the Moslem practice of slavery from that given by those who feared and hated Islam as a powerful religious force. On the other hand, they would have sounded like dangerous nonsense to hundreds of thousands of Christians who had fallen into the hands of brutal masters. These unfortunates would have reminded the apologists of how they had been driven in chains to the slave markets where the bystanders spat at them, called them 'infidel dogs', and allowed the children to throw stones at them. In the market itself they were handled and examined like cattle. Their eyes and teeth were inspected; their chests, arms, and legs were prodded; they were made to run up and down like horses to test their wind. The young women were immediately marked down as the booty of the local monarch, which was tantamount to life imprisonment in vast and gloomy seraglios; and from what evidence we have, there was very little Arabian Nights 'romance' in such a fate. Men fit for hard work were sent either to the galleys, or assigned to those vast building projects which the megalomaniac rulers were for ever undertaking, for thousands were required to demolish the old palaces, often destroyed out of sheer jealousy of the reigning monarch for his predecessors; while more thousands were needed to build new palaces to replace them. And in almost every street of the cities of Barbary Europeans could be seen harnessed to carts like draught horses or selling water from jars loaded on the backs of donkeys. Those who were not seen were worse off still, for they were toiling as labourers or carters under the whips and scimitars of the overseers who lashed them on to their feet if they fell down from exhaustion. Of the enormous numbers of Christian slaves in Barbary (there were 25,000 in Algiers alone in 1634), only a small proportion were as fortunate as Vincent de Paul.

As if in confirmation of the official indifference to these unfortunates, almost the last act of the drama was the affair of Caroline, Princess of Wales and subsequently queen to George IV. For while Princess Caroline was being delightfully entertained by the Bey and organising excursions to Carthage and other pleasant picnic spots, Lord Exmouth, commanding nineteen British and six Dutch ships of the line, was bombarding both Algiers and Tunis and forcing the royal lady's host to sign a treaty abolishing the enslavement of Christians throughout his dominions. When the Tunisian monarch abruptly terminated the festivities, and the Princess with her friends were obliged to leave, the royal lady expressed her extreme displeasure that politics were permitted to interfere with her social calendar.

In contrast with the indifference or unwillingness of the British to put an end to piracy and its evil consequences, the Americans, from the inception of their republic, reacted with justifiable indignation to this gangsterism on the high seas. Before their independence, they had enjoyed no more security under the British flag than small nations like Denmark and Sweden who relied wholly on the payment of tribute for the protection of their interests. Indeed, American ships were being captured in the Atlantic only five years after the Pilgrims landed at Plymouth Rock. They continued to be harassed so disastrously during the colonial period that interference with American commerce was conceivably one of the reasons for the War of Independence. At any rate, we find a New Englander writing in November 1680:

> The Turks have so taken our New England ships richly laden homeward bound, that it is very dangerous to goe. Many of our neighbours are now in captivity in Argeer (Algiers). The Lord find out some way of their redemption.[1]

The implication, of course, is that the British Government was disinterested in the fate of its transatlantic subjects.

It was even worse after the war, for the Americans had no protection at all on the seas for the next two decades. In 1783, for instance, no fewer than ten of their vessels had been picked off by the Barbary pirates and their crews sold into slavery. Benjamin Franklin, *en route* to France as the first American ambassador, was feared lost, 'taken by the Algerines'. In fact,

1. Charles Sumner, *White Slavery in the Barbary States*, 1853, p. 70.

Lloyd's of London refused to insure American ships at all which, as a result, had great difficulty in obtaining cargoes. The Mediterranean and the Atlantic off the south European and African coasts were, to all intents and purposes, closed to American trade.

This serious blow to their economy, together with a genuine patriotism natural to a young nation which had just obtained its independence by the sacrifices of a small population, caused great indignation among a still resentful and bellicose people who regarded the Barbary pirates as neither more nor less than 'human harpies'. Accounts were continually published in the newspapers of the sufferings of American captives at the hands of their Moslem masters. One Bostonian was said to have been chained to a wheelbarrow for eighteen months and allowed only one pound of bread a day. Another slave, this one a Philadelphian, was harnessed to a plough with a mule. Others were chained to oars in the galleys.[1]

It made no difference that these Americans were simple sailors; their fellow countrymen, on reading of such atrocities, were outraged, all the more so as they were impotent to do anything about it. Yet no American, whether politician or private citizen, was prepared to tolerate a *laissez-faire* policy vis-à-vis piracy. To the contrary, the issue became a national crusade. First, Benjamin Franklin in Paris shrewdly enlisted the aid of the Trinitarians—no mean feat in view of the traditional anti-Protestant prejudice of this order. Next, American agents boldly turned up in the pirates' lairs and called at the beylical palaces with the greetings and full-length portraits of President Washington, already an international hero. However, when it came to talking business, the Barbary monarchs were adamant: there were set prices for ransoming slaves and no amount of flattery or cajolery could prevail on them to give the Americans favoured treatment. We have an exact listing of these prices for the year 1786.[2]

1. *Boston Independent Chronicle*, May 18th and October 16th, 1786. Vol. XVIII, No. 916; Vol. XX, No. 1042.

2. Theodore Lyman, *The Diplomacy of the United States*, 1826, Vol. ii, p. 353.

Master of a vessel	$6,000
a mate	4,000
a passenger	4,000
a seaman	1,400

These, then, were the ransom fees the Bey of Algiers was asking in 1786. What the agents were authorised to offer was $200 per American, irrespective of his status. This sum, though pitifully small, was the limit of what the new Congress could afford, since there were 115 known American captives in Algiers alone, with several hundred others scattered up and down the Barbary coast. At $200 per man, therefore, the total needed was in the region of $50,000, whereas the rapacious Bey was demanding ten times this sum.

But the American public refused to be dismayed and at once set about finding ways and means to raise the ransom money. Colonel David Humphreys, Washington's old comrade-in-arms, suggested a national lottery; a special Sunday was allocated as a day of prayer and fund-raising; and Congress itself allocated the remaining funds. As soon as the money was available, the United States entered into negotiations with the Bey of Algiers, and a treaty was drawn up whereby the young republic not only agreed to buy back its citizens but also to pay an annual tribute in order to ensure the safety and freedom of its nationals on land and sea. The cost to the American Government and people was $700,000, an enormous sum for those times, but one which was spent, as Washington himself said, 'as a special subject of joy to every feeling heart'.

Shortly after this, a second 'peace' treaty was signed with the King of Tripoli in which the Americans paid $50,000 for the purchase of their enslaved citizens in that territory. This treaty, incidentally, contained an article which is probably unprecedented in the diplomatic history of the United States. Article Two expressly states:

> The Government of the United States is not in any sense founded on the Christian religion.[1]

1. Lyman, op. cit., Vol. ii, pp. 380–1.

The national rejoicing attendant on these so-called peace treaties was short-lived. The pirates were not awed by either the Bey of Algiers or the President of the United States, and it was not long before they were attacking American vessels, including the occasional warship they caught off the African coasts. Colonel Humphreys again expressed the national sense of outrage, this time in verse:

> Where am I? Heavens! What mean these dolorous cries?
> And what these horrid scenes that round me rise?
> Heard ye the groans, those messengers of pain?
> Heard ye the clanking of the captive's chain?
> Felt ye the blood, with pangs alternate rolled,
> Thrill through your veins and freeze with deathlike cold,
> Or fire, as down the tear of pity stole,
> Your manly breasts, and harrow up the soul?[1]

Colonel Humphrey's appeal was answered with action. The Government sent a squadron of warships to bombard Tripoli and sink the pirate ships, but the frigate *Philadelphia* ran aground on a reef and her crew of 300 officers and men were captured, manacled, and thrown into prison. It cost the Americans $60,000 to ransom them.

By 1815, however, the Americans were finally in a position to act. They sent a strong force into the Mediterranean, settled accounts with both the pirates and rulers of the Barbary coast, negotiated the release of all American captives without the payment of ransom, and signed treaties that never again would citizens of the Republic be enslaved.

The following year the British, acting for the first time in concert with other European powers, decided to follow the Americans' example. Lord Exmouth was despatched with nineteen British and six Dutch ships-of-the-line to the Mediterranean. In the meantime, a troopship, the *Prometheus*, had been sent ahead to smuggle out the consul-general and his family before the bombardment of Algiers began. The ladies of the party were successfully escorted aboard the rescue ship disguised as midshipmen. A marine carried a basket of fruit

1. David Humphreys, *Miscellaneous Works*, 1790, pp. 52, 53.

and vegetables in which was concealed the new-born baby of the consul's wife, a Danish girl not yet sixteen. Passing the Turkish guard at the sea gate, the baby began to cry. As a consequence, the surgeon, three young midshipmen, and the boat's crew of fourteen men were arrested and thrown into prison. The baby, however, was sent to his mother aboard the *Prometheus*, which then sailed off.

A few days later the Anglo-Dutch armada arrived off Tunis and reduced that city to impotence by twenty-four hours of bombardment, much to the annoyance of Princess Caroline, as we have seen. From Tunis Lord Exmouth sailed to Tripoli, which received the same treatment. Thus, within a space of ten days, piracy was, to all intents and purposes, ended as an organised activity in the Mediterranean, though many regretted its decease, including those whom Lord Exmouth refers to as 'the old mercantile interests'.

And so ended Christian slavery in Africa with the American naval victories of 1815 and those of the Anglo-Dutch in 1816. The principal ports of the Barbary coast, the lairs of pirates in Salé, Tangiers, Algiers, Tunis, and Tripoli, had been bombarded into subjection and the corsairs driven from the seas. The slave markets where the remark had often been heard 'Christians are cheap today' were closed down; the infamous *bagnios* were filled in; and the iron hooks once attached to every city gate for the exhibition of the decapitated heads of slaves and malefactors were removed. The Christians, indeed, were shortly to exact a full retribution for the wrongs done them by the Moors by occupying every Barbary state for the next 100 years and more. From the point of view of the Moslems, Christians were now enslaving them, only the process was now called colonialism. Colonialism, in turn, has been replaced by nationalism, but whatever system obtains, slavery in some form or the other still flourishes throughout the continent.

EPILOGUE

The Emerging Continent

Our knowledge of Africa is so slight compared with our long and detailed records of the West that we tend still to think of its inhabitants in almost the same terms as the historian Pliny described them nearly 2,000 years ago—as an assortment of tribes living in a state of near-savagery. Because of this subconsciously arrogant view, the entire continent and its several hundred million people were, until recently, considered of no importance in the world of international politics. Very few natives, in fact, had a voice in the councils and conferences held by the great powers to decide the issues of the day, including the future of the Africans themselves. As subject peoples, they did what they were told even to the extent of fighting wars of whose origins and objects they had not the slightest conception.

How different the scene is today! And consequently, how difficult it is for Western politicians and people alike to accept or understand the rôle of nearly forty recently created African states, all with some kind of government, civil service, armed forces, police, and political objectives, the whole complex nominally independent of, and increasingly hostile to, Western hegemony. For what we see of Africa today is a bloc of politically, socially, and economically unstable nations which ape the institutions of the West without having had either the time or the experience to absorb them, while using these institutions—the vote in the United Nations is the prime instance—to exploit the fears and rivalries of the white nations. We see, too, that, internally, native opportunists have seized power, and they call themselves prime ministers, or presidents, and control parliaments and courts in an often ludicrous parody of democracy. Yet democracy, a concept which has little meaning outside the West, is a sort of talisman, as if the repeated utterance of the magic formula will solve all problems and the theory of 'one man, one vote' will turn the Africans into a modern, freedom-loving, democratic people.

The hard facts are quite different. First, Black Africa is still tribal in its social and economic structure. We haven't thought in terms of tribes in Western Europe for 1,000 years; the ordinary African, even in North Africa, cannot think in any other terms. The tribe is his nation; the chieftain his prime minister; and the village council his parliament. Secondly, he feels no involvement with his national parliament, because even if he has the vote, he hardly knows whom he is electing to represent him. Thirdly, the administrations and assemblies of almost every African state consist of men who have either usurped or bought positions of power, and over whom the masses have no control whatsoever. The only rivals to the current leaders are other opportunist politicians, rich men, and army officers. Fourthly, women still have no opportunities in government, so that half the population has no voice at all in the running of affairs. Such a political system cannot be called democracy; and the West may well be wasting its time and money in trying to impose our institutions on new nations who have no intention of adopting them.

These, then, are the facts. Where the student of modern Africa has to be careful is how he interprets them. The quick and specious conclusion is that Africans are unfit to govern themselves because of their ignorance of our methods, their intellectual inferiority, lack of education, and political inexperience. One hears it sometimes stated in support of this opinion that the Africans have never advanced beyond the Iron Age and, in the case of some tribes, not even as far as that. According to this line of argument, the artistic and technological achievements of the Negro are insignificant compared with those of the Western or Far Eastern civilisations, since the Africans have produced little in the way of art or architecture other than the Benin bronzes, which some claim are the result of Portuguese skills, or the Zimbabwe monuments, which others assert are of Arab origin. Nearly all the other artifacts belong to the culture of a primitive people whom the Romans, not as apt as we are to mince words, called savages.

Yet, here again, we should remember that classical observers like Pliny knew nothing of prehistory—or, rather, conceived of the dawn of mankind in terms of myths: whence they assumed that the Africans had always been savages, and were therefore incapable of intellectual and artistic achievement. This belief has died hard, like the idea that Stone Age Man was an ape-like creature who inhabited caves and lived a brutish existence, devoid of any refinement. But the discovery of rock engravings and paintings throughout Africa should change our view of the Negro's intellectual potentialities, as the discovery of European cave art changed our view of his white contempories. Both races appear to have developed along the same lines in the beginning; and, as far as attainments are concerned, there seems little to choose between them. In fact, there is an extraordinary similarity between their art, almost as though they had the same teachers and styles, as well as the same ideas, in common.

Yet the fact remains that civilisation, as we understand it, developed more rapidly in the West (and one includes the Middle East in this general concept of Western culture) than it did in Africa, though this phenomenon does not conflict with the thesis that the Africans were potentially capable of making the same progress, given the same favourable conditions. We base this suggestion on what evidence is available, visual evidence on the rocks all over Africa that demonstrates how the Hunters evolved into Herdsmen and Herdsmen into Agriculturists—the same progression as that of Western civilisation. At this stage of evolution, the Africans stopped, or sank back into either barbarism or savagery; and we can only speculate as to the reasons.

One obvious reason was climate, which favoured the Middle East, the Mediterranean basin, and southern Europe and condemned the Negro race to inhabit a continent of desert and forest. The difficulties of bare survival left no time for intellectual pursuits, or the leisure for art, philosophy, and science. We have seen what physical conditions can do to stultify a people in the case of the Dawada; and the lesson is repeated in the case of the Bushmen of the Kalahari Desert. Obviously, the mental effort necessary to produce all the artifacts associated with civilisation are impossible in the middle of a desert or, for that matter, a jungle. It was partly environment, then, and not the innate inferiority of the Negro race, that prevented Africans from creating a civilisation comparable with that of the West or of the East.

A second reason for their cultural delay seems to have been the invasions of the white race, one instance of which has been discussed here in the chapters on the Garamantes. We have drawn the inference that the two cultures—the white culture based on martial superiority, the black on cattle-herding and agriculture—could not both survive. The probability is that the Garamantes destroyed the emergent Negro civilisation by enslaving the aboriginal population, a process that was repeated by the Romans in their fashion and by later conquerors in theirs. It follows that native cultures under these conditions of continual invasions and occupations had no chance of developing along their own lines.

We can assume, therefore, that these two factors—an adverse environment and the impact of more advanced white civilisations—prevented the aboriginal Africans from evolving beyond the stage of a primitive cattle-herding or agricultural society. The striking intellectual and artistic potential of both their rock art and hydraulic works was never to be realised; and it is now no longer profitable to speculate as to what level of civilisation they would have risen if they had been left in isolation, like, for instance, the Mayans and Incas before the Spanish Conquest.

On the other hand, there were whole areas of Equatorial and South Africa which did remain outside the influence of the West right up to modern times, and we are forced to admit that these remote kingdoms or tribal communities showed few signs of social evolution. The first explorers could not describe them as other than primitive, if not outright barbarous, characterised by appalling cruelty, superstition, and ignorance. Climate and white invasions could not be blamed for this state of affairs: hence the question is bound to be asked why, in such cases, the Africans, when left to themselves, hardly advanced beyond the Iron Age. Must we fall back on the argument that the Negro is intellectually inferior to the Caucasian?

Two aspects of this study of lost African worlds may throw some light on this problem.

The first of them is the record of Christianity in Africa, occurring in three clearly marked phases: the first during the Roman period, lasting from about A.D. 100 to A.D. 700; the second the period of the Portuguese-Spanish evangelisation, A.D. 1550 to A.D. 1780; and the third, the modern period from 1800 to the present. Our conclusion has been that the Christian gospel at no period ever took a firm hold on the Negro mind, to the detriment of the African people themselves. In suggesting this, however, we are not asserting the superiority of Christian dogma so much as emphasising its civilising effect. Thus, no one would deny that Christianity, where it practises what it preaches, humanises society, and certainly did so in the case of the Roman world where its influence was first felt. We have noted that the Romans, who were so uncompromising about the nature of barbarism and savagery, were barbarians and savages in much of their treatment of their fellow men and that it was the early Christians, Africans like Tertullian, Cyprian, and Augustine, who protested against these inhuman practices and eventually saw them abolished or mitigated through the agency of the Church. So, too, during the Middle Ages, the cult of chivalry arose from the basic concept of Christian mercy and charity; and, in our own times, Christianity was the operative force behind the abolition of slavery.

Never having become Christianised in great numbers or with great conviction, the Africans were deprived of the humanising and civilising influences which, more than anything else, contributed to the formation of Western society.

Those who did accept the Gospel of Jesus Christ too often did so out of expediency to make much difference to the general welfare. In fact, judging from the missionaries' own reports, many of the converts kept one foot in the old African world of animism, witchcraft, and superstition. Those, on the other hand, who embraced Islam, did so partly under duress. The remainder clung to the ancient tribal gods.

The result was that there has never been one unifying spiritual force in Africa to elevate men's minds or improve their social conditions. The Christian converts were ineffectual, largely due to their lack of conviction. The Mohammedans accepted a creed which, in its strict interpretation, opposes social and even technological change, as the continuing bondage of women in orthodox Moslem society demonstrates. So with the Africans who remain pagans: their gods and cults are unquestionably inimical to progress, for they are the emanations of prehistoric man's terror in the face of natural phenomena. Fundamentally they have to be placated by blood and murder, and their distinguishing characteristics are cruelty, intolerance, and despotism. It is axiomatic that men must civilise their gods before they can become truly civilised themselves, and the Greeks took good care to do this with a god like Apollo, who originated as the Killer and ended as the Life-Giver. The African pagans never civilised their gods, but remained their fear-stricken subjects, a fact which must be taken into account in examining the question of why they were still savages when Europe was at the zenith of its civilisation.

These considerations have a bearing on the backwardness of much of Africa and help to explain why slavery has always been endemic to the Dark Continent. Having nothing in their religion to interdict the individual's right to inflict cruelty, the Africans saw no ethical, let alone practical, reason for abolishing slavery, even in its most inhuman aspects. Nor did Islam give them a very different view of either the value or the sanctity of life, since the Prophet authorised the enslavement of the infidel. The failure of early Christian evangelisation was largely due to the Church's having made the same mistake of ignoring the Negro's humanity, thus jeopardising for centuries its opportunity of being the vital spiritual force which could have expedited the civilising process in Africa. If, in addition, we remember that the Christian participation in the African slave trade was followed by colonial exploitation, we understand better why the continent has been so slow in developing.

All of these factors, generalised and vague though they seem, are relevant to the fundamental question as to whether Africans are capable of relinquishing their tribal past and of creating what we regard as civilised nations, not in the material sense alone, but, far more, in the spiritual, moral, and social sense. As in the case of all primitive peoples, this means an enormous psychological change, far greater than that needed to learn how to drive a tractor or service a car. It means, for instance, the abolition of all forms of serfdom not because of international treaties or pressures from outside, but because of an interior conviction. It means, too, the liberation of women, the abandonment of cruel and senseless tribal customs, and the rejection of the old fetishes and the mumbo-jumbo that surrounds them. In brief, profound social changes must precede political progress and, for that matter, the introduction of technological aids by which Western reformers set so much store.

The dangers are obvious. For what we see in other parts of the world which are also making the transition from savagery or barbarism to Western civilisation is often a rejection of what is good in the old culture and an acceptance of what is bad in the new. This is nowhere more apparent than in the conflict between the attitudes and manners of African city-dwellers on the one hand and the people of the oases and villages on the other. The former have already acquired much of the materialism and opportunism characteristic of Western urbanism; the latter still retain the antique virtues of the desert and forest. The younger generation who migrate in increasing numbers from the rural communities to the slums of the semi-Westernised cities are in great haste to become outwardly Westernised, but the impression one gets is that they are discontented with the old order without desiring to create a new and better one.

For this reason the future of Africa is impossible to predict. We can only be certain that great changes lie ahead as the old ways of life disintegrate and the continent emerges into the twentieth century. Compared with the problems of the future the 'lost worlds' which we have glimpsed in this study are already ancient history. Yet it is hoped that it has been worthwhile recording them in order better to understand some of the unseen forces which continue to operate behind the façade of modern Africa.

Bibliographical Notes

As no attempt has been made in this book to give more than a few glimpses of African history, both ancient and modern, a general bibliography is not included. In any case, the subject is so vast that such a list, even of comprehensive histories, would be impractical. Those students, however, who wish to investigate some particular aspect of African life are referred to the relative bibliographies, encyclopaedias, and reference books. They will find *Africa: a Handbook to the Continent*, edited by Colin Legum and *Africa: Its Peoples* by George Peter Murdoch, especially useful.

BOOK ONE

CHAPTERS ONE–THREE

The total literature on the subject of the Dawada would make a volume of not more than a score or so of pages, since this Libyan tribe has only been reported on by the few European travellers who have managed to reach them in the course of the last 140 years.

Dr. Walter Oudney, the Scottish explorer and the first European to see them, stated nearly all we know about these 'Worm Eaters' in his monograph *Excursion to Westwards of Mourzouk*, included as a prefix to the celebrated *Narrative of Travels and Discoveries in Northern and Central Africa by Major Denham, Captain Clapperton, and the Late Doctor Oudney* (1822). This book and its authors are discussed at some length in *The Great Sahara* (1964), Chapter 8.

Oudney's successor, Dr. Eduard Vogel, the German explorer commissioned by the British African Association to work with Dr. Henry Barth, made a quick excursion to the Dawada in 1855.

Vogel died in Africa, but a résumé of his findings can be found in the *Annales des Voyages* (1858), edited by V. A. Malte-Brun.

Henri Duveyrier, the young French explorer, was the next to visit the Ramla el Dawada, and his report is contained in his classic *Les Tuareg du Nord* (1864), where he calls the famous 'worms' *Arthemia oudneii*, in honour of the Scottish explorer who first described them.

The 'Worm Eaters' then disappear from the records for the subsequent seventy years, until the Italians occupied Libya and made the first scientific studies of the people and terrain of the Fezzan. Their findings, including some data on the Dawada, are published in a series of monographs contained in a volume entitled *Il Fezzan* (Governo della Tripolitania, Ufficio Studi, No. 1, December 1932).

Additional material will be found in G. Caputo, *Il Sahara Italiano: Fezzan e l'oasi di Gat* (Bollettino della Reale Società Geografica Italiana, 1936); E. Zavattari, *Sul Duda: il cosi detto verme comestibile* (Reale Istituto Lombardo Scienze e Lettere, Fasciculi I–IV, 1935); and C. Gini, *Inchiesta demografica, antropologica, e medica sui Daudi del Fezzan* (Bollettino Geografico del' Ufficio Studi, Tripoli, 1937).

During the short French occupation of the Fezzan a scientific mission spent some time in the vicinity of the Wadi el Ajal and produced a valuable report, particularly regarding the geological phenomena of the Ramla el Dawada. The student is referred to *Mission au Fezzan*, published by the Institut des Hautes Études de Tunis (Publications Scientifiques, No. 1, 1953), where the findings of the geologist Dr. Pierre Bellair are of special interest.

A fascinating sidelight is also thrown on the Dawada in Colonel Limouzin's 'La Marche chez les Daoudadas' in the *Bulletin de Liaison Saharienne* (No. 5, June 1951). The French traveller Philippe Diolé gives a vivid description of his visit to the 'Worm Eaters' in his *Dans le Fezzan Inconnu* (1956).

BOOK TWO

CHAPTERS FOUR–SIX

The systematic study of rock art is scarcely fifty years old, and since the engravings and paintings found on cliffsides and in mountain caves cover a period of at least 40,000 years in almost every inhabited part of the globe, it follows that we are still a long way from recording, let alone analysing and interpreting, all the material both known and still to be discovered.

There is, however, now available a number of general introductions to the subject for specialists and non-specialists alike, among which may be noted: G. Baldwin Brown, *The Art of the Cave-Dweller* (1932); Leo Frobenius, *Prehistoric Rock Pictures* (1937); Allan Houghton Brodrick, *Prehistoric Painting* (1948); Henri Breuil, *Quatre Cents Siècles de l'Art Pariètal* (1952) and *Cave Drawings* (1954); Paolo Graziosi, *Palaeolithic Art* (1960); and *The Art of the Stone Age* (1960) by various authors. Each of these books lists a bibliography.

The number of full-length books, monographs, and articles dealing with special aspects of rock art in various parts of Africa now runs into hundreds, and the student who wishes to pursue the subject will be best advised to consult the bibliographies appended to the latest publications. Thus, Fabrizio Mori, in his *Tadrart Acacus* (1965), lists some 200 references, mostly pertaining to North Africa. For the remainder of the continent, Ingrid Rosenkrantz's *Rock Paintings of South and Central Africa* provides a comprehensive bibliography.

The first traveller to report the existence of rock engravings in Africa was Dr. Félix Jacquot, whose *Expédition du Général Cavaignac dans le Sahara Algérien* (1849), pp. 149 ff. has been consulted. Reference has also been made to Leo Frobenius and Douglas C. Fox, *Prehistoric Rock Pictures in Europe and Africa* (1937); Henri Lhote, *The Search for the Tassili Frescoes* (1959); Agnes Susanne Schultz, 'North-West Australian Rock Paintings' (*Memoirs of the National Museum of Victoria*, No. 20, 1956); and Paolo Graziosi, *Palaeolithic Art* (1960).

Since no useful study of African rock art can be made without an examination of the pictures themselves, the following books are recommended for their excellent illustrations: G. B. M. Flamand, *Les Pierres Écrites* (1921); H. Obermaier and H. Kuhn, *Bushman Art* (1930); Leo Frobenius, *Ekade Ektab* (1937); Paolo Graziosi, *Arte Rupestre della Libia* (1942); W. Battiss, *The Artists of the Rocks* (1948); Yolande Tschudi, *Les Peintures Rupestres* (1956); Henri Breuil, *The Rock Paintings of Southern Africa* (1957); Jean Malhomme, *Corpus des Gravures Rupestres* (1959); and F. Mori, *Tadrart Acacus* (1965).

The best collections of African rock pictures, which are continually being added to as travellers report new finds, will be found in the Leo Frobenius Institute of Berlin and the Museum of Man in Paris.

BOOK THREE

CHAPTERS SEVEN–NINE

No one has yet attempted a formal history of the Garamantes, since almost all the evidence of their Saharan empire still lies buried beneath the sands. Indeed, until the Italian archaeological expedition of 1933 surveyed the Fezzan, little was known of this mysterious people except for an occasional reference in the classical histories. The first mention of them is found in Herodotus, after which their name appears but rarely in the contemporary Roman records. What references there are are listed in the dictionaries and encyclopaedias of Greek and Roman writers, and none of these tells us very much.

The source book for what information we have is still the *Scavi Sahariani* (1951), in which are published the archaeological and anthropological findings of the Italian scholars who surveyed the Wadi el Ajal, the main artery of the Garamantes.

The work of the Italians was continued after the 1939–45 war by individual archaeologists, and eventually a small British expedition began work around Germa, the Garama of classical times, capital of the Garamantes. In the meantime Dr. M. S. Ayoub, Controller of Antiquities for the Fezzan, continues his excavations and the classification of the immense amount of pottery still being brought out of the tombs and graves. A small museum in Sebha, the modern capital of the Fezzan, houses the principal finds of the various digs made over the last thirty years.

The Italian anthropologist Sergio Sergi is the principal exponent of the theory that the Garamantes belonged to the white race and that the Tuareg are their lineal descendants. Professor Sergi reached his conclusions on the basis of his study of the skulls of dead Garamantes and of living Tuareg. His data, arguments, and findings will be found in *Scavi Sahariani* and in various articles listed under his name in the British Museum catalogue.

Also consulted in connection with the present author's discussion of the Garamantes were Orin Bates, *The Eastern Libyans* (1914); Francis Rennell Rodd, *People of the Veil* (1926); and Louis Adolphe Hanoteau, *Essai de la Grammaire de la Langue Tamachek*.

A gap of over 1,400 years lies between the Garamantian empire of A.D. 500 and the survivors (if such they are) of this people in the persons of the Tuareg. For most of this period, we have only the records of the early Arab historians, notably Ibn Khaldun. It is Ibn Khaldun who gives us the last description of the once-famous nation whose king surrendered ignominously to Okba ibn-Nafi in A.D. 669, after which the Garamantes disappear into the mists of history, unless, as we have suggested in this account, they survive in remote enclaves of the Sahara which they once undoubtedly controlled as confederates of Rome.

BOOK FOUR

CHAPTERS TEN–THIRTEEN

The whole field of early Christianity in Africa has been thoroughly recorded and documented both in the works of the Christian Fathers themselves and in the researches of modern Church historians.

The most informative, as well as interesting, accounts will be found in the works of the early commentators themselves, some of whom were prolific writers, notably Tertullian and St. Augustine.

The principal contemporary sources, then, are the *Apology* and *De Spectaculis* of Tertullian; the *Confessions* and *Letters* of St. Augustine; the *Octavius* of M. Minucius Felix; and the writings of various bishops, historians, and polemicists like St. Optatus, St. Cyprian, Herodian, Porphyry, Diodorus of Sicily, and others who witnessed and commented upon the rise of the African Church.

General histories of the period by modern scholars include: C. J. Tissot, *Géographie Comparée de la Province Romaine d'Afrique* (1884–8); A. Toulotte, *Géographie de l'Afrique Chrétienne* (1894); Charles Diehl, *L'Afrique Byzantine* (1896); H. Leclercq, *L'Afrique Chrétienne* (1904); Abbé Leynaud, *Les Catacombes Africaines* (1910); A. Toulotte, *L'Afrique Chrétienne* (1912); and Cabrol's *Dictionnaire de l'Archéologie Chrétienne*. Also consulted with reference to the persecutions of Christians in Roman Africa were the articles: 'Les sacrifices ordonées à Carthage au commencement de la persécution de Decius', by C. Massevieau in *Revue de l'Histoire des Religions* for January–February 1884; and 'Les Inscriptions de Chemtou' by A. J. Delattre in the *Revue Archéologique* for April and June 1881 and May and October 1882.

The following books were also consulted: E. Amélineau, *Les Moines Égyptiennes* (1884); P. Alard, *Le Christianisme et l'Empire Romaine de Neron à Théodore* (1897); J. M. L. Besse, *Les Moins de l'Orient* (1900); Charles Dubois, *Étude sur l'Administration Romaine* (1908); F. V. M. Cumont, *Les Religions Orientales* (1929); E. G. Hardy, *Christianity and the Roman Government* (1925); and H. M. D. Parker, *The Roman World* (1955).

The four volumes of Charles Pelham Groves's *The Planting of Christianity in Africa* (1948–58) were found especially valuable for their factual summaries of almost 2,000 years of evangelisation; and Dr. Diedrich Westermann's *Africa and Christianity* (1937) was a useful theological guide.

The account of Ramon Lull has been compiled from the *Catholic Encyclopaedia* and E. A. Peers, *Ramon Lull* (1929).

Acknowledgments are made to W. H. Bentley, whose *Pioneering in the Congo* is a fascinating account of Central Africa at the beginning of this century.

For the nineteenth century the writings of the missionaries, both Catholic and Protestant, have been consulted.

The World Christian Handbook and the periodic reports of the various evangelical societies provided such statistics as are available for a continent where no precise census has yet been possible.

BOOK FIVE

CHAPTERS FOURTEEN–FIFTEEN

African slavery is, of course, too vast a subject for any one book to deal with adequately, all the more so as it has always been an integral part of the social and economic life of the entire continent, whence the actual slave trade, as engaged in by the European nations, is only one aspect of the institution. The procedure adopted in this survey, therefore, has been to confine the account within the limits set by several of the principal source books for our information of the nature and extent of slavery and the slave trade.

The following books and pamphlets have been found especially useful: the *Travels* of Sieur Germain Mouette (1708); Thomas Thompson, *The African Trade for Negro Slaves* (1772); James Ramsay, *Essay on the Treatment and Conversion of Slaves in the British Sugar Colonies* (1784); Thomas Clarkson, *The Cries of Africa* (1821); the books and letters of the nineteenth-century African travellers and missionaries; and the reports of various governments and international organisations, notably the League of Nations and the United Nations.

Eyewitness accounts of the treatment of prisoners-of-war and slaves by Africans themselves have been taken from Eduard Vogel, *Reisen in Central Afrika* (1859); Dr. E. Ruelle, 'Notes anthropologiques sur quelques populations noires de l'Afrique Occidentale Française', *L'Anthropologie*, 1904, pp. 680 ff.; Dr. Heinrich Barth, *Travels and Discoveries* (1890); René Caillié, *Travels through Central Africa* (1839); James Richardson, *Travels in the Great Desert* (1848); and Hanns Vischer, *Across the Sahara* (1910).

CHAPTERS SIXTEEN–SEVENTEEN

The first history of white slavery in Barbary is Father Pierre Dan's curious *Histoire de Barberie* (1649). As a Trinitarian, Father Dan was as much concerned with propaganda as with the facts, for in his day Christianity and Islam were at outright war with one another. Father Dan's book, therefore, should be read in conjunction with Paul Deslandres's *L'Ordre des Trinitaires pour le Rachat des Captifs* (1903) and Calixte de la Providence's *Corsaires et Redempteurs* (1892).

An interesting Protestant view of the question by an American will be found in Charles Sumner, *White Slavery in the Barbary States* (1853), a valuable source of facts and figures concerning American captives. Sir R. L. Playfair has done much the same thing for British slaves in his *The Scourge of Christendom* (1884).

An essential aspect of the study of white slavery in Barbary is piracy, since the vast majority of Christians sold in the markets of the North African ports were taken on the high seas by the corsairs. The following histories have been consulted: Jurien de la Gravière, *Les Corsaires Barbaresques* (1887); Stanley Lane-Poole, *Barbary Corsairs* (1890); Juan Cabal, *Piracy and Pirates* (1957); and Robert Carse, *The Age of Piracy* (1959).

The description of conditions in the galleys of ships during the age of oars is taken from Admiral Jurien de la Gravière's *Les Derniers Jours de la Marine à Rames* (1885).

The accounts of their experiences by individual slaves who returned to their homeland and wrote their story are especially valuable to the historians of North Africa, though their books have long been out of print and are now available only in the national libraries. The following list represents a short bibliography for students who wish to investigate the subject further: Sieur Germain Mouette, *Relation de la Captivité* (1708); John Windus, *A Journey to Mequinez on the occasion of Commodore Stewart's Embassy* (1725); Henry Boyde, *Several Voyages to Barbary* (1736); Thomas Pellow (edited by Dr. Robert Brown), *History of the Long Captivity* (1740); Thomas Troughton, *Barbarian Cruelty: or an accurate narrative of the sufferings of the British captives belonging to the 'Inspector', privateer, during their slavery under the Government of Muley Abdallah, Emperor of Fez and Morocco* (1751); Mrs. Crisp of Minorca, *The Female Captive* (1769); Charles Smith, *The Ancient and Present State of Cork* (1774), which gives an account of the corsairs' raid on Baltimore in Ireland; Georg Höst, *Nachrichten von Marokos* (1781); John Nicholl, *Some Account of the Worshipful Company of Ironmongers* (1886); and Louis Abelly, Bishop of Rodez, *Vie de St. Vincent de Paul* (1888).

Particulars concerning Charles I's dwarf, Captain Sir Jeffrey Hudson, will be found in Frederick William Fairholt's *Eccentric and Remarkable Characters* (1849) and in the *Dictionary of National Biography*. There is a painting of Sir Jeffrey by Daniel Mytens at Hampton Court and a Vandyke portrait of Queen Henrietta with the dwarf at Petworth House in Sussex. His waistcoat, breeches, and stockings are in the Ashmolean Museum.

The following books have been found helpful both for their factual information and their bibliographies: C. M. MacInnes, *England and Slavery* (1934); Sir George MacMunn, *Slavery through the Ages* (1938); E. W. Bovill, *Caravans of the Old Sahara* (1933); F. D. Lugard, *The Dual Mandate* (1923); and the bibliographies of Morocco and Algeria compiled by Sir R. L. Playfair.

Index